The Education of a Doctor

MY FIRST YEAR ON THE WARDS

John MacNab

SIMON AND SCHUSTER · NEW YORK

Any similarity to a large metropolitan medical center is purely coincidental. (That goes for the people too.)

All rights reserved
including the right of reproduction
in whole or in part in any form
Copyright © 1971 by John MacNab
Published by Simon and Schuster
Rockefeller Center, 630 Fifth Avenue
New York, New York 10020

First printing

SBN 671-21017-3
Library of Congress Catalog Card Number: 71-156158
Designed by Eve Metz
Manufactured in the United States of America
by American Book-Stratford Press, New York, N.Y.

This book is dedicated to Madi, who once asked
*"What
do you do
in a day?"*

Admissions Note

"And whatever I may see or hear in the course of my profession, as well as outside my profession in my dealings with men, if it be what should not be published abroad, I will never divulge, holding such things to be holy secrets."
—HIPPOCRATES, *"The Oath"*

This journal will cover my third year of medical school, and the name MacNab will do as well as any other. I am atypical in that I had a late conversion to medicine, whereas most of my classmates grew up in this faith. I had considered and rejected careers in a variety of other fields, including organized religion, painting highways, teaching dead languages, and the law. I had met people in each of these fields who were very unhappy. Medicine looked interesting and undeniably worthwhile, and the few doctors I knew seemed to like it.

I went for it.

I had one year of undergraduate work left before I would have to convince the medical schools that I was a suitable candidate. This promised to be a charade of heroic proportions. My liberal education had led me away from the sciences: my one concession to distribution requirements had been to take a course in the history of science, where I had learned that these scientific people have a tradition of being almost right. So I set about my year of premed courses with real fear (because of poor preparation and no talent) and a sense of adventure.

It worked. I told the medical schools I wanted to be a G.P. It was the year that the magazines discovered that the country needed more G.P.'s. I got in.

The first two years of medical school were an extension of college without any of the fun of undergraduate life. Lectures and exams in windowless amphitheaters provided the mixture of boredom and fear that is considered essential to a really good education. Besides the white jackets, only two things set you apart from your former classmates: your solid draft exemption and your cadaver in anatomy lab.

This coming year looks like the start of the real apprenticeship. I will be in the hospital attached to our medical school for the first time, rotating through each of the services. As the junior assistant to the intern, I should see a panorama of practical medicine and take a voyeuristic peek at life.

There is bound to be another opinion on the subject of divulging "holy secrets." I will change the names, dates, and other details, but the charge can still be made. My apologies to anyone who wants them.

I think it's worth recording.

Pediatrics

June 9, 1969

My first day in pediatrics. I would have preferred to start in obstetrics for the sake of the form of this journal; as it is, that will be my next service, forcing me into hysteron proteron all summer long. Our group of five were introduced to the house staff * and shown around the wards. First patient pointed out to us had encephalocele—the bones of the skull did not close right and the cortex of the brain extends through the gap. We were told this was fatal, nothing we could do but wait until the patient succumbed to an infection. Decided this baby's condition symbolized our time. A resident then asked what would happen if we cut off the projecting cortex. Answer: the same thing as cut off the whole cortex—NOTHING. Like all newborns this baby was operating at a "subcortical level"; he was using the lower, more primitive parts of his brain. Also a symbol of our times.

* House staff: the interns and residents; i.e., the salaried hospital physicians.

Trotted after the house staff to a lecture on phenobarb and neonatal jaundice. By Greek doctor, who observed sets of babies in Athens and Lesbos. Nice slides of Lesbos.

In preceptor group later we were shown a movie on the development of reflexes from fetus through infancy: we are well programmed for sucking and for hanging on to the shaggy skins of our parents. Just as with all previous lectures and didactic movies, I retained nothing I should have.

My third year really started when I got back to the ward. Was on duty last night, which means I had to write up new admissions. Derek Kinney came in at four. Blond baby, one year old, reminding me of the infant at the climax of *2001*. Silent! Has a rare condition (first described about ten years ago)—a catchall syndrome involving the kidneys and the blood. The intern came up with the diagnosis by listening to his "history" from his mother and learning from a nurse that his urine was pink. Maybe yes, maybe no, on prognosis. I explained to the parents (intelligent, glasses-wearing, *N.Y. Times*-reading) that this was my first day in clinical medicine; they misinterpreted this to mean my first day in medical school but took it well. I was embarrassed to have to elicit from them the illnesses in their family. The father described his mother as a "paranoid schizophrenic" and their "social condition" (a modest garden apartment in the suburbs: "humble origins" their word for it). May have been too flippant and casual in my questioning in view of the baby's prognosis (a sign of my nervousness). My contribution to his treatment—doing clotting time tests (we were treating him with anticoagulants) and cutting and pasting EKG strips in his chart. Trivial responsibilities, but I could not shoulder larger ones at this stage.

A second patient came in at midnight named Flora Santos. Little baby (one month old) with big, swollen abdomen. Her mother had taken her to a local hospital

36 hours ago for fever, diarrhea and vomiting. The belly had swollen since then. The other hospital did not know whether to operate or not, so transferred her to us.

The mother was 23, short, with a holy peasant face. She was like a 10th grader in a parochial school—not yet interested in lipstick. I am sure that many rosaries had been said. The father was 21, a handsome young Latin with lively eyes. He walked down the ward as if strolling through a bar, glancing around for his friends and smiling at every face that met his. He spoke no English, and smoked nonchalantly as his wife gave the history of his daughter's illness. It was as if she were negotiating the repair of a refrigerator: he was consulted every so often, but he had already budgeted the cost. Unconventional, but a good man.

We didn't know what was wrong. We called down a surgical team to look her over, and had X-rays taken. Consensus was it could be a number of things: intestinal obstruction, perforation, appendicitis, kidney cyst that ruptured, cirrhosis, . . . the list went on. After some deliberation we decided to tap the peritoneal cavity. A dilute, pink fluid came out, not very illuminating. We were pretty sure the baby would live through the night, and were going to wait for the morning to do more tests for the diagnosis; we were frankly stumped.

A surgical intern removed an IV catheter which the other hospital had inserted near the groin, and noticed the same dilute bloody fluid came out. His first reaction was that he had punctured the peritoneum (the saclike membrane that surrounds the intestines). Then he did some thinking, because he had enough experience to know he had been too careful to make such a mistake. What if the catheter had been placed (by the other hospital) not into the vein but into the space around it and thru the peritoneum? Then the fluids and blood transfusions would have gone not into the circulation but would be sitting in the abdominal cavity. We did a quick test on the hypothesis. We knew the baby's blood sugar was normal; if the fluid was from the infusions (which include dextrose) it might be expected to be very much higher. A one-minute paper strip test showed the fluid's sugar to be roughly twice normal. Bingo! Great elation among the five medicos who had sweated over the problem. The night was ours. The surgical intern was very modest, trying to give credit to the others for suggesting the possibility. I kicked myself for not thinking of it.

This meant the baby would not need surgery that night, and we could slowly draw off the fluid with a needle. Next big problem: should we tell the parents? Their daughter was off the critical list; with a minimal explanation that news seemed to satisfy them. These two patients consumed my night. Went down for seven o'clock breakfast. Fantastic first day on the wards.

June 10

I was supposed to "present" these two patients to the other doctors and students at "rounds" this morning. Presentation consists of recounting the history, physical, tentative diagnosis, and "management" of the patient— i.e., what we had done for him. Botched the job. I was very tired (previously at med school I had gone to bed at eleven and I was unaccustomed to "all-nighters") and the two cases intertwined in my mind (many similar symptoms; tough to remember which one had a cold before diarrhea, which one vomited after). Also because I am garrulous. The resident then cautioned us about the need for concise presentation, the danger of tangents, etc. (Wrong, I thought: a tangent at least has a point in common with the circle; my lines were not even in the same plane). I will have to work on this, but how? I could go back to elementary school and perfect my elocutional circles in "show-and-tell." I think my trouble is that I never had to "show-and-tell." I have spent the last ten years writing papers and talking to friends. My time in the classroom has been spent *listening* to lectures or presentations (while making asides) and in small groups "contributing" to the discussion (or rather detracting from it). I hope I can now become an automaton—unhesitant and direct.

June 11

I was given some responsibility today and blew it. The resident asked me to draw a blood sample from Derek (the pt [patient] on anticoagulants) for a clotting time. I wisely made sure his parents and grandmother were not around, assembled my equipment, put on a gown, and went into his room. There I was confronted with a tangle of intravenous solution tubes and pumps whose complexity called for a consult with a master plumber. I "traced the wires," closed valves, and detached some lines, drew some blood out from a line in the ankle, placed it in the test tube. But on reconnecting the system, I broke a coupling. I asked the student nurse (they should never put two students together alone) to get me another. She went and told the head nurse, who yowled in disbelief. I was informed that there might not be another replacement part in the whole medical center. She started calling other wards, trying to track one down. Time was moving, and this was a time-dependent test. Luckily my roommate happened onto the ward. I gave him the tubes to do the test fast. A nurse came up from another floor with the wrong part. I called the head nurse in and she saw that the part required was actually a simple one and fetched it from a closet. By this time the resident came in (on my "May-Day") and we worked on the repairs. My roommate reported a clotting time of 5 minutes. This was much faster than we wanted or expected. (We were aiming at 20 to 30 minutes.) At my suggestion we tried to draw some more blood to repeat the test. But I couldn't get any blood to flow with either pressure or a vacuum in the syringe. "You know, we may be in trouble," said the resident. If the blood in the catheter had clogged, we would have to pull it out and get a surgeon to insert another (a process that had taken the surgical resident over an hour last night). Luckily the resident was able to get the flow restarted by pushing in some saline with a syringe. The resident was nice about it, and criticized not my mistake but my reluctance to reinsert the new coupling (I was trying to ward off the second bolt of lightning in the same place). I have a new respect for plumbers.

June 12

I did a little better today. I had to add 5 ml of sodium bicarbonate to Derek's IV. It is a hospital rule that the family should not be present when the patient is being treated; even under the most skillful hands the patient often reacts badly (from wailing on up to anaphylactic shock). Another reason for this rule is the possibility of less skillful hands and downright incompetence such as mine yesterday. ("No point in needless alarm.") But as the family got up to go, I told them they could stay. It was a foolish gamble, but they knew I was inexperienced, and would be "needlessly alarmed" at the idea of me alone in a room with a needle and their only child. This was a simple procedure; if I botched it though . . . They were curious about what I was injecting; I showed them the label on the bottle. "You know, sodium bicarbonate." Jokes about hangovers. With their eyes watching every drop, I added the 5 ml without a hitch. Gambled and won.

With new confidence I went to draw some blood from Mrs. Santos. Her daughter's big belly had subsided and

Mrs. Santos wanted to take her home, but we wanted to keep her in the hospital to check out the history of GI disturbances and present anemia and undernourishment. Sounds cold-blooded of the doctors, but we were afraid that the child would continue to "fail to thrive." We had little confidence that the mother would be quick to seek help for a problem of this subtlety, and even less confidence that her local hospital could solve it. We wanted the blood to investigate a possible ABO blood-group incompatibility which would have occurred in pregnancy but might explain the present symptoms. (I see, I've been brainwashed already: I believe.) "You think I might have given her some disease?" the mother asked when I told her I wanted to draw blood. I mumble something about infection and incompatibility, trying to avoid the possible guilt feelings in either case. Mrs. Santos is too close to the fields, I now realize, to become neurotic about her daughter's disease. But I am glad I kept it vague; there was nothing for her to misunderstand. She followed me docilely into the treatment room, where I performed the venipuncture like a pro.

June 13

We meet with our preceptor every afternoon for a seminar on pediatrics. I like these meetings. Our preceptor is an Olympian figure, as many senior men appear to third-year students, and even a nice guy. He is wise enough not to try to teach us anything. Instead, he assigns topics and cases and has us present them to the group; he "clears up points," but never "lectures." Another thing I like is that he demands an informal description of a case in our own words: correct, robotlike presentations are discouraged. A good learning experience, with eager learners.

The topic was "Early Development." I was assigned the case of a 2-year-old boy with mongolism who was on another floor. Not an especially ugly child, but his features were large and slack. He had developed normally for the first few months, but fell behind the pack: at 2 he cannot stand unaided, let alone walk. In the hospital for corrective surgery of his insides. As I left his room, a woman asked me if I had wakened him. His mother, who loves her son. Sincere embarrassment, which I tried to mask with concern. I asked about her son's development ("How old was he when he first . . ."). Cooperative, painful responses, and the dread explanation. "You know he has mongolism, but they say he's one of the better ones." Courageous woman. I felt like a heel.

June 16

Two newborns. The first: "Baby Doe." Some boys were playing baseball in the street and heard some funny "meows" coming from a trash can. A baby girl, covered with garbage, umbilical cord cut but not tied. The infant on the mountain. Slum goddess. She was sent to our emergency room, where she was informally christened "Michele," and sent on up to our ward. Nothing especially wrong with the girl, who will be kept for a few days and sent on to the Department of Child Welfare. The intern could not resist calling the admitting resident and telling him to stop sending us his "Puerto Rican trash." I'd like to give her a trust fund. With a provision for a debutante party.

The second little girl was born in the hospital two days ago. I went to see her mother, who was an old friend of mine. The baby was fine; I was more interested in talking to my friend and her mother. They had known me since prep school, and had a harder time than most people in picturing me as a doctor. They questioned me about my responsibilities with interest and polite skepticism. I illuminated for them such details as where I got my white

Pediatrics

coats cleaned (I had a blood spot on my collar). I was grateful that I had not started on obstetrics. I will never be able to treat anyone who knows me. It is not only our mutual lack of confidence, but also that I like my friendships to be uncomplicated. We talked about reading in the enforced leisure of the hospital. No enforced leisure for me, but this afternoon was very civilized. Glad to keep it on that plane.

June 17, 18

Took the National Board exams, Part I. These exams are very useful for certification in most states. This part covered the material from the first two years, and I may have blown a fuse in my mind reviewing the bulk of it in two days. I realize now that this stuff is relevant and that I should know it as well as a Jesuit theologian knows his Aquinas. On the other hand, if the right answer exists in books, I can always look it up. Maybe.

The exams were like running through a line of clubs—success was not in the picture, I just wanted to get through alive. They were of the multiple choice type, or rather "multiple guess." Agony over each of the 900 questions: after eliminating the impossible answers, choose between the remaining improbables, uncertains, and unknowns. Photographs of slides with all the definition of polished granite. I could barely determine the organ, let alone the lesion. In the last part, though, the examiner must have realized that unless there were 50 "gift" questions there would be an acute shortage of doctors in 1971. Enjoyed answering puerile puzzles such as "DNA is found in the (a) cytoplasm, (b) nucleus . . ." I still may not have passed, but I can retake this series until I do.

After the first day of exams I decided that it was pointless to study for the second part. Went to a movie, having failed to get a date on the spur of the moment. That is the major annoyance of this apprenticeship: the difficult social life. Every other civilian bachelor contemporary has his evenings off in which to try to amuse himself along these lines. They may not succeed, but the opportunity is there. Tougher for this kid (a) as a medical student in pediatrics on duty every fourth night and with "homework" each night for the preceptor groups; (b) as a *poor* medical student: like a lot of my classmates I have a part-time job; I work as a blood chemistry technician every fourth night for another hospital; (c) as a *poor, tired* medical student: when I discover I am free, my thoughts lift heavenward to the sack. It is hard to plan dates, and "bullet" invitations often backfire. On my rare dates I am likely to feel that I have squandered my evening off on someone who does not appreciate and is unworthy of my sacrifice. My problems will all be solved when I meet a beautiful heiress with a prescription for benzedrine.

June 20

A patient on our ward was operated on today. A 3-month-old boy born with the pipes of his heart joined the wrong way. The only reason he has survived this far is because of another major defect: a hole between the two sides of his heart. Usually surgeons like to wait until a child is 6 years or so before a major operation, but in this case they had to move faster because of the possibility of brain damage from continuous oxygen-poor blood.

I went up to visit him in the "open-heart recovery room." Controlled bedlam. Eight beds in the room, separated by a maze of portable curtains—like walking through a bazaar. A muscular young woman being sponged; a boy and a girl (brother and sister?) awake and watching TV from their beds ("I Spy"); an old woman in pain repenting her existence; and the baby. The operation had gone well enough, and things looked hopeful. A heavy, blonde nurse took temperature, respiration, pulse, and blood pressure every five minutes with all the dumb efficiency she had doubtless displayed in keeping the frankfurters coming fast last weekend. A sweet and homely lady MD monitored the respirator and the EKG oscilloscope. The surgeon had dropped by, and also my resident. I was pressed into service to do a hematocrit;* this showed the baby needed a transfusion, so I volunteered to fetch the packet from the blood bank.

I left the room with a sense of exhilaration. Never in my life had I been in a place where so many expert people were working full time. (This is the only part of the hospital where the coffee percolator is going round the clock.) For peak efficiency it had some of the elements of an aircraft control tower and a short order cookery. Steady, regulated adrenaline.

When I returned the picture had changed: the oscilloscope showed that the heart was failing, the baby was being respirated through a balloon bag, and the dapper surgeon had a worried look and was slightly annoyed. Evidently the baby had suffered an arrhythmic attack. We tried various procedures, calmly, but to no avail. I saw the baby's eyes glazed like a fish. I suggested we give him digitalis to boost his CO (cardiac output). The others said no: the rate, already low, would go down, and there was always the danger of arrhythmias with the drugs. I argued that we had nothing to lose and should act while

* Hematocrit: the percentage of the blood volume that is occupied by red cells. A blood sample is taken by a fingerprick: you draw the blood into a small capillary tube, stopper it with a plug of white clay, centrifuge for five minutes, and read the proportion of the sedimented red cells. This percentage goes down acutely when there has been internal bleeding; it should be maintained at a certain level with transfusions. The hematocrit can be chronically low with a failure of production of red cells, as in iron deficiency, or with hemolysis, as in sickle cell anemia. (I must have done five zillion hematocrits this year.)

we still had something to win. They agreed I had a point, but stuck with their present drugs, saying that digitalis would provide only a temporary effect and would not help the deeper trouble, whatever that was. (Had the sutures burst? The baby was bleeding internally.) It was their experience versus my textbook impressions and impatience. Appeals with an analogy to "the gambler's last roll"—but no dice. I left to get some supper and some sleep. Found out the next day that the baby had died—the time given was before I left. The parents refused to allow an autopsy. I don't blame them. I was told we probably would not discover anything from it anyhow. So it goes.

June 24

We switched this week to another floor with slightly older children—more like *putti*. I like the change. The staff is more low key: it includes a fourth-year student with the title of "subintern," an intern who looks and thinks like the "GI Joe" toy soldiers—always stands "at ease" on rounds, legs spread apart, arms clasped behind him, staring attentively and vacuously just beyond you—and a kindly "attending physician" of late middle age who breaks into smiles even more frequently than I do (he from good nature though). Instead of doing battle with cardiorespiratory physiology after rounds, we dealt with the practical problem of what to feed infants. Given: you are in charge of an infant orphanage in Vietnam with crates of US foodstuffs, make up a formula. Answer: Condensed milk comes in 13-oz cans—dilute to 1 qt volume and add 2 tbsp of sugar. The scientifically approved kiddy elixir. A good thing to know. I can't wait to start boring people with this.

Went to a party tonight given by college friends, or at least acquaintances. One had been in classics with me, but was now in law. We rejoiced that we were no longer in classics (*Erudition:* Dust shaken out of books and into empty skulls—Ambrose Bierce). He asked how I liked medicine; I was noncommital, not feeling up to an account of my joys and sorrows in that field. The other law student was a different matter: his father was a doctor, and he was very much under the influence of his father's ideal. He had tried premed courses at college, but had done so miserably that he had decided on law. I too had done miserably in premed courses, but they only confirmed my vocation. (MacNab's law—do what you're worst at—a corollary of the Peter principle).

When he asked me about medical school I replied as honestly as I could: that it was a tremendous work experience but an empty private life. I invited him to come up, put on a white coat, and observe from the inside. He is too fine a person to be envious of me, but he did seem to wish he could have done what I did. For my part I was pleased to have a prize that someone wanted, but I am not sure how much I want it for myself. I envied him for being free to get married and live a pleasant *New Yorker* kind of existence, but I suspect he may end up in medical school yet.

June 25

On duty again tonight. A little boy was brought in because he had swollen up yesterday and his urine had appeared dark brown. I interviewed the Spanish-speaking mother through an interpreter, his aunt. Jorge Cruza had come down with a cold two weeks ago. A classic case of poststreptococcal acute glomerulonephritis (or Bright's disease) which I had studied earlier to present to our afternoon seminar. Quick tests confirmed the diagnosis which sounds worse than it is—90% of the kids recover in 3 weeks with no aftereffects. Had a tough time straddling the fence: I wanted to relieve the mother of her anxiety but at the same time cover ourselves (and divine providence) in case the child was one of the unlucky 2% who get the chronic disease. Did an adequate job for once—thank God I had been forced to learn up on this.

Another boy was admitted for part of his periodic anticancer therapy. He had an abdominal tumor, inoperable, but was improved by certain drugs. As a result of these medications, he was bald—almost, with only a fine peach fuzz on his scalp. It may be my knowledge of his destiny, but he struck me as very mature—a man-boy, shirtless, in black overalls. Active, polite and well-behaved, he commanded my respect. Because of his prognosis I wanted to indulge his boyish appetite by, say, a trip to the Wild West; his Gandhi-like maturity, however, suggested he should be Secretary-General of the UN. He was less than and more than a saint. I was slightly antipathetic to cancer research before on the grounds that the money could be better spent on public health projects such as population control. I feel a little differently now.

June 26

After rounds I went to the funeral of a friend, an old man who had enjoyed life and done good works and died suddenly of a stroke. Mixed emotions. A long and healthy life is what this business is all about, and this man had taken full advantage of it. In the hospital I get the impression that deaths don't matter, that the human race will take care of itself. Interesting to find out that my professional "tough hide" (which may be a sham) does not apply to my friends. I wept.

June 27

Spent my "free" time today writing up my Clinical Clerk's Admission Note on Cruza, the mama's boy nephritic who was back to normal after two days (but still needed watching). This note is part of a medical center's obsession with information, most of which is irrelevant to curing the patient now but which may or may not be useful for his treatment or to some researcher at a later date. I find it embarrassing to ask the mother about all her pregnancies (they assume my interest lies in criminal abortions) and their living conditions (where, how many rooms, does the baby have its own room, do the grandparents or another family share the apartment, and what does the child eat for each meal). I find the section on "Development" ludicrous: I have to learn at what month the child "First Smiled, Pushed Up, Sat Without Support, Stood Without Support, Walked Alone, Spoke Single Words (Q. Does 'Mama' count?), Sopke 3-Word Sentences, and Had His First Tooth." The mother guesses her way through most of the list (baby Cruza must have spent his first four months scowling at the world). Then there often is the language barrier, which forces me to demonstrate "pushing up." One feels a fool—this must be the hazing of the profession.

The physical exam is a torrent of trivia. You start with a tape measure and, after the height, get the head circumference, chest circumference, abdominal circumference, and (crowning imbecility) the ratio of the distance from the crown of the head to the pubis and from pubis to the sole of the foot. Actually, these numbers can indicate that the child is not growing up right, but they always seem pointless at the time. Three things are especially tough to examine on children. With the lungs, the chest is too small to percuss unless you have the hands of a midget, and you can never get the child to take a deep breath and hold it, say "99" ten times, whisper "one, two, three." The heart is difficult also because of limitation of space and because it is beating at almost twice the adult rate. Using the ophthalmoscope on "real people" is hard enough—a trick I have yet to master, but at least you can get them to hold their gaze. Infants show no such cooperation; they try to close their eyes and swivel their eyeballs around like searchlights at an airport. Thus a cursory eye examination can take an expert half an hour, while you wait, cheek to jowl, for the fidgeting child to "flash" his central retina onto your screen. I can distinguish glass eyes from real ones and that's about it.

At the end of the report you have to make a summary: "Briefly in one or two telegraphic sentences summarize the history and physical examination." This is a good intellectual discipline: you are forced to compress the preceding logorrhea into a couple of pellets. These "telegraphic sentences" are all the information that is really needed for treating the patient's chief complaint.

Then comes your "Impression," i.e., tentative diagnosis, which is readily obtained from the intern or the nurse. By consulting a text in the relevant area you should also put down a list of other possible diagnoses to be "ruled out" (although they are rarely all excluded; it is more often a case of one of the diagnoses fitting so well that it settles onto the throne, and the pretenders are forgotten). Finally "Procedures Recommended," i.e., for treatment. At this stage of my training I do not know any therapy I would recommend for an enemy's sick dog, so I leave this section out of my write-up. It has never been missed.

June 28

An intern presenting the case of a leukemic stated that a certain symptom is *never* seen in the childhood form of this disease. The old "attending," who has made a specialty of this sad field, gently reminded him that *"never* is a long time."

June 29

We are not all required to make "rounds" on weekends, as long as one of us is there or "on call" for admissions. I put in a token appearance and found a very relaxed ward. Sat around drinking coffee with the subintern and third-year student on duty. Topic of conversation: the AMA. The other student is mustachioed, and SDS, and has as much love for the outfit as Pancho Villa had for the landowners. The subintern is more moderate; he is about to inherit some land. "Fighting the AMA is a career in itself: you will never be able to practice medicine." Stick to your farm. Pancho sweats with patient rage.

Went to see a college roommate off for Greece with his new family. He plans to live there for a few years: he is blessed with a modest independent income and an incisive lack of ambition (he is rejecting an academic career in philosophy, reasoning that Life Is What You Live). This may seem like lotus-eating, but I am sure my friend will continue to grow in wisdom and in knowledge. If I were to do this, though, there would be no such progress. I envied my friend for his indifference to the demons that drive me—the need to justify my life. The road not taken. I wonder if I will later have the honesty to rue not taking it.

July 1

On duty tonight—the inevitable admission, Susan Rome, was brought in by her grandmother because unusually sleepy, unusually silly, acted "drunk." The little girl said she had some whiskey, but we had to rule out meningitis. I watched the intern do a spinal tap—negative—and then interviewed the mother. Assumed the man she was with was the father—wrong, actually the "stepfather." They both worked at a state mental hospital so they had last seen her asleep this morning. Seemed perfectly well yesterday. Couldn't understand where she got hold of some liquor. Some sleeping pills at home, but these all accounted for. Upset. I told them their daughter would probably be fine tomorrow though she might have a hangover. I was annoyed at them and the girl for making me go through the procedure of a CC Admission Note, when it was obviously a case of too much booze. I could not smell alcohol on her breath, and the resident remarked that the story sounded odd.

We gave her no treatment, just monitored her asleep and did some tests. One of these tests paid off—it disclosed the presence of "ketones" in the urine. There were three possibilities: aspirin, acetone (often found in acidosis), and phenothiazine (a central nervous system depressant). Blood tests for the first two left only the third, which was made more likely by the fact that the patient's mother worked at a mental institution, where the drug is widely used.

July 2

Little girl was normal this morning. Confronted the mother with our tentative diagnosis of phenothiazine intoxication. "I don't know where she could have gotten one of those pills." I decided not to press the matter. If she had been trying to fool us, she must have a new respect for us now.

Another patient came in this afternoon. I was not on duty, and called up the student who was "Pancho Villa." I later regretted pulling him from his dinner when I found out about the patient. This boy had been brought to the ER (emergency room) for some stitches above the eye (he had fallen). The resident had given him a sedative to facilitate the operation, but had given him the dose for a full-grown man, thus knocking him out. The boy was admitted to the hospital for "observation." The resident would not want any admission note on him, and especially not one written by Pancho Villa.

July 3

Pancho exceeded my expectations. On rounds this morning, when the attending asked about this patient's chief complaint, Pancho answered "An iatrogenic * overdose of sedative!" We all laughed. The attending was good-natured, though, and asked why the student was so sure this was the true cause. "Because the resident told me so." More laughter. The attending then opened the chart to Pancho's admission note, and was alarmed to learn that the patient's chief complaint was *on the record* as "iatrogenic overdose." A serious lecture followed.

The attending had exquisite shoes and a kindly face. He is one of the few doctors in the hospital that the kids like and the parents trust as well. In the first place, he pointed out, the chief complaint should be just that: an explanation, in the patient's words, if possible, of what brought him to the hospital. It was not supposed to be a diagnosis, or even an "Impression." Thus, the words "iatrogenic overdose" had no place there. Attending advised recopying.

In the second place, how could the student be so sure that it was this "overdose" that accounted for the patient's present condition. Had he seen the patient before admission? Had he ruled out the possibility of cerebral hemorrhage as a result of the fall, or meningitis, intoxication, and hypoglycemia?

In the third place, the attending continued patiently,

---

* "Iatrogenic" means "induced by the physician." It is a key word.

there was the legal angle. If the patient's father decided to sue the hospital over this case, for whatever reason, then his lawyers could request a copy of the chart. This request would have to be met. When the lawyers received this copy, and saw the phrase "iatrogenic overdose," in the first sentence to boot, their eyes would open wide, and they would say, "OH, BOY!" (the attending's face radiating joy to drive his point home). The hospital could be sued at any time in the next 14 years. The state statute of limitations specifically exempts pediatrics cases from the normal 7-year deadline, extending the liability till the patient reaches 21. The attending had sat on this hospital's malpractice board for a number of years. He had seen the hospital lose $100,000 over a sliver of flesh from the third left toe. He knew of four doctors on the staff whose estates were now tied up because of such suits.

"And finally, I'm the attending who is liable in this case, so I'm *ordering* you to change that note."

The student took this well, admitting that he had chosen the wrong field of battle for the attack. After rounds the subintern called a meeting of the third-year students on the ward. He told us that he often got just as mad as Pancho but that he believed in "reform from within." Then he chewed us out for not knowing the normal range of values for each laboratory test: this was mainly directed toward me, for I had questioned him earlier about a figure for WBC (white blood cell) count, asking him if it were high or low. The meeting ended with a discussion of the morality of not charging this family for this visit. Some students said that it was too much like a bribe. My sense of probabilities told me that a bill would be sent, that it would not be paid, and that would be the end of the matter. I straddled both sides in silence.

I found a comic conclusion to the whole affair later that day. Jorge Cruza (the mama's boy with nephritis) periodically refuses to drink anything, and this is bad. Instead of feeding him IV, we pass a tube through his nose into his stomach and send some milk through the tube. Then he eats regularly for three days or so. Not too attractive, but it works. This time, I made a final attempt to get him to drink his milk. No go. "That's what comes of a permissive upbringing," the nurse explains. "You know, they did a study of the college protesters and showed that they all had permissive upbringings." I will pass this on to Pancho.

July 7

A new fortnight, another ward. Even more low key. This appreciation is more than just the release from the tensions and frustrations of each previous ward. This time I have hit the bottom. The attending has been inveigled from his research on fluid balance in the newborn. He stands with arms folded and one hand on his throat, trying to appear interested in what's going on, but more often mildly amused. One intern is obviously impatient with the finer details of university hospital medicine and is eager to get out, get some money and some sleep. The other intern reminds me of the hero of *Goodbye, Columbus* —he would be just as happy to work as a librarian in Newark. His great love is his magnificent file of articles from medical journals. The resident alone keeps the ward going; a Virginian, he tries to communicate the feeling that there is a lot to be done in a little time, but that it must be done right or not at all. He drives hard. He is not averse to shifting to neutral, though, to give us the lowdown on such arcane subjects as the importance of finger and palm whorl patterns in diagnoses of certain genetic diseases ("One of the coming things in medicine"). I discover I may have an ogrelike chromosome defect, but I clench my hand so no one will suspect.

On specialty rounds we discussed the treatment of a boy with leukemia on our floor. I was familiar with the patient's history: last month I had "presented" him briefly to our preceptor group. At that time I was not on this floor, and I went up to what I assumed was a doctor outside his room and introduced myself as a third-year student who was assigned to make a report on the case. The man in white shoes replied, "Pleased to meet you— I'm his father." I was ashamed of myself for my enthusiasm about "the case."

July 8

Spent this morning drawing blood out of other people and having it drawn out of myself. There is one set of tests for clotting studies that is a true pain: it requires blood not only from the patient under scrutiny but also from a "control." The control is a volunteer. We jokingly tried to con the nurses into it, holding their arms up to the light and praising the beauty of their veins, but no go—they said they were specifically exempted from this sacrifice. I then offered myself—I have terrific bulging bricklayer's vessels on my arm (and like to show them off). We went into the treatment room, taking the whimpering patient. To make him feel better about the whole affair, we told him that I would go first to provide an example of stoicism. I had to be more stoical than I bargained for. My colleague, who aspires to a career in molecular biology, manages to miss my veins. (He told me later that he didn't realize that veins could "roll.") I had to sit there while he poked around with the inserted needle, hoping to strike oil. He finally hit the pipeline, but passed right through so that a golf ball swelled under the skin. The patient, who was only an observer, started wailing. My colleague, sweating and apologizing profusely, tried again on the other arm and missed again. Back to the original arm for strike three and out. I took out my rage by working on the patient, hitting the vein on the first try, while my colleague held him down and reassured him. Back to my arm for the control, and success. The yellow-purple "hematoma" marks will last a week. I was annoyed at the other student for his weakness: I have had no more experience than he but can get my needles dead center by a triumph of the will.

A patient with a massive shoulder tumor was brought in to die. This girl's cancer had been diagnosed in Puerto Rico, and the doctors told the mother that with surgery she had a 5% chance of living another 5 years. The mother talked it over with her daughter and decided that these odds were not worth the loss of an arm and a breast. The girl returned to school, and the tumor swelled and eroded the bone. I was invited to view it with the bandages off if I "wanted to see something really sickening." Rejected the offer. I did go into her room to help start an IV. The girl was a beautiful young woman—a Madonna patiently awaiting the Assumption. Pathetic "Get well soon" cards lined her wall. The mother also a beautiful young woman. Austere in her sorrow. It was easy to see how they made their decision—for them ugliness was worse than death. They could have gone one step farther, though. The room stinks of infection every time you pass it. Dying is also worse than death.

July 9

When you switch floors you are "assigned" a couple of patients: you are responsible for following these as well as the ones you "admit." Bruce Black was, as his name denotes, a Negro boy, with a bulging left eye that made him look like something out of *Pogo*. He was going to be operated on today for a biopsy, and I was in a hurry to examine him so I could write an On-Service Note. Read through his chart—the swelling could be caused by inflammation, cancer, or even a parasite, and I managed to examine his eyes just before he was rushed off for his preanesthetic. Tried to figure if one eye was worth an arm in the chess game of surgery. Later I scrubbed-in to watch his operation. Emerged from the locker room looking like a spaceman—white PJ's, cap, and mask, with black plastic bags around my feet. The surgeons look even more 21st century with a face mask made of turquoise fiber and shaped like a rudimentary proboscis. I was impressed at all this fuss taken over this little boy from South Carolina. The biopsy looked courageous: they sawed the bone to the side of the eye to relieve the forward pushing pressure. Pogo's ocular globe stared confidently and magically through the bloody proceeding, fearing no evil. The surgeons found a mass behind the eyeball and took some slices, then closed up the face. Twenty minutes from first cut to last stitch. I will look at the slide next week to learn if Pogo's confidence is justified. I suspect it is— the surgeons said it didn't feel malignant and we learned today that it had previously shrunk on treatment with steroids. I hope we all are lucky.

July 10

Assisted today at a renal biopsy for the other patient I had been assigned. Julio Roya is a little Puerto Rican boy who developed "the nephrotic syndrome" * 5 years ago after an operation to remove a congenitally defective part of his large bowel. He was subjected to a colostomy— which means that his lower GI (gastrointestinal) tract empties into a little bag attached to his abdomen. Twice he was readmitted to see if he was ready for the next operation, which would return his body process to normal. Each time his kidney condition precluded surgery. The nephrotic syndrome is characterized by protein in the

* The nephrotic syndrome might be described as generalized swelling secondary to a chronic kidney disease.

urine and low protein in the blood, along with a high cholesterol. The patient swells up: Julio looked like a Sumo wrestler. He was intelligent, but his whole personality disintegrated at the prospect of having blood drawn or even a Band-Aid removed. His chief fear, I learned, was that someone would remove his bag. I wonder if his condition is psychosomatic: as long as he had this nephrosis the surgeons were not going to touch his bag or otherwise mess around with his precious excrement.

My first duty in this biopsy was to get written consent from a parent. Felt like an encyclopedia salesman: the form was a blanket one, with "Renal Biopsy" written in one corner, the printed text granting us full power over her son's body and any parts we cut from it. The mother signed immediately—buffaloed by my white coat and sense of urgency. Actually this biopsy is probably more for our benefit than Julio's, although it will tell us if he has a disease which is easier to treat than his present diagnosis.

Down in the biopsy room, a big dose of sedatives had failed to lessen Julio's apprehension, much less put him to sleep. We had him lying face down on an X-ray table, and reassured him while the doctor put needles in his back. After the local anesthetic he couldn't feel much, but was still fearful—it was a good thing he could not see the instruments. I tried to divert him with a game. I would press a coin onto his leg and ask him to identify it by the feel. The doctor put in a probe needle and was directed by his colleagues who were watching the X-rays on a TV set in the next room. When he came to insert the biopsy needle, I pressed a quarter against Julio's calf and said, "What is it?" Julio was wrong, but we got our biopsy and could stop needling him.

Worked as a chemistry technician tonight at the other hospital. Not much to do as usual. Did a set of electrolyte tests on one lady in heart failure. She was hooked up to an oscilloscope, and I had the thrill of seeing her bigeminy (two different alternating waves) change to normal series rhythm within ten seconds after injection of a drug. A close friend of mine was monitoring another patient—an old lady with terminal breast cancer, in a stupor and close to the finish line. She may have suffered a stroke. My friend demonstrated no less than six subtle pathological reflexes, naming each as he went along. (He did have his little black notebook open at the bedside.) The old lady didn't seem to mind; she never said a word.

July 11

Another admission—a possible repeat of Bright's disease. Pedro Moderno had trouble from the instant of birth. The mother said that when he came out he was blue; she was immediately put to sleep and was not allowed to see him for the first week. Home for a month, then back to the hospital for pneumonia for another three months. Came to our hospital at the age of 8 for convulsions stemming from his heart defect, which was partially corrected by major surgery. This latest incident came a week after tonsillitis—it looks like AGN (acute glomerulonephritis) but could be associated heart trouble or a number of other things. He is on the waiting list for complete corrective surgery—and if the present illness is not too severe we may try to sneak him in.

Spent half an hour trying to get his pulse. I hadn't realized that his heart operation cut down the arterial flow of his left arm. Pedro was big and fat and dull. He was as patient as an animal in a zoo: this gave him a curious nobility. Tough to examine because of his fat and retardation. His heart sounded like 42nd Street. At midnight I cut short my "complete physical examination" and let him go to bed.

Examined his urine through a microscope. Red cell cast—pathognomonic of a glomerulonephritis. Just what he has time and the tests will show. And then?

Pediatrics

July 14

Drew a half-dozen tubes of blood from Pedro for diagnostic tests. Much blubbering. "You're going to do it hard." "No, Pedro, I will try to do it soft" (whatever that means). "If you are good, I will let you bring your radio along." Pedro promises to be good and clutches his transistor. I hold the wheelchair steady. Pedro faces it, puts his left foot on the opposite pedal, and has to pirouette on it like a circus elephant before he can sit down. I wheel him down to the treatment room, and this he enjoys. I hoist him to the table and ignore his cries as I apply the tourniquet. "You're doing it hard." This is the easiest part, Pedro. I search for a vein—his skin is like a water buffalo's. To divert him while I search, I try to start a general conversation. It turns out that Pedro knows even less about baseball than I do, and that out of our common heritage of Western civilization, our only point of contact is horror movies. Pedro's face lights up in an account of Dracula—I concentrated on his veins. (I have drawn blood from the external jugular before, but his was not visible, and Pedro has enough problems with reality as it is.) I select a candidate in the arm, drive the needle home, and start filling the syringe. Pedro bellows with pain and fright. I tell him the worst is over, and I am nearly done. "Just count to ten." Through his sobs he answers, "I can't," and his wails increase. He is 12 years old.

July 15

I presented a patient to the head of the department today—an exercise we are called on to perform once in our rotation. I selected Derek Kinney—my first patient, the one with the rare kidney syndrome. For the first time I understood what we were trying to do for this patient and what we had accomplished (Derek had left after a month's stay with the three main features of his syndrome back to "within normal limits"). His case makes the hospital look as if it works. I had all the figures written down before me, and had practiced my talk. No stutters or embarrassing pauses. If nothing else, in six weeks I have improved my ability to talk about Derek Kinney before a group. I am satisfied with my progress.

July 16

We admitted a patient who was one of 13 children—on the basis of a history from the mother. This child had been in before and had been discharged without a diagnosis— we couldn't find anything wrong with him. I put forth my theory that the mother had too many kids to handle and was using the hospital as a hotel. Nothing like a grab bag of "complaints" to tantalize a university medical center into a quest for an underlying disease.

One intern (the one who reminded me of *Goodbye, Columbus*) added the following story to this discussion: "When I was upstate we had to watch out for guys who would say anything to get into the hospital. This would become obvious with the right questions—once we had a guy who responded affirmatively when asked: 'Do your knees knock?' 'Do your teeth itch?' 'Does your shit glow in the dark?'"

July 17

I was on the emergency ward service tonight. Resisted asking questions about stool fluorescence. A lot happens, but there were no real fire alarm emergencies, thank God: the worst case was a broken ulna. One boy came in moaning softly, unable to talk, his hands up by his shoulders. "Phenothiazine toxicity," said the resident. A neurologist confirmed it: we gave him a recently discovered antagonist (for an overdose of a recently discovered drug) and within four minutes the boy was talking normally and had his arms relaxed. Dramatic reversal. We dismissed the parents casually, knowing their confidence in the medicine men will never be shaken after this miracle. Just tell it to the tribe.

The rest were all the same. I learned that being a busy pediatrician is not difficult. The mothers will bring their kids in with a history of low fever, vomiting, and diarrhea, and a variety of other symptoms. First rule out meningitis (check for a stiff neck and a few other signs), then say, "Viral gastroenteritis." No one can prove you wrong. Treatment requires nothing stronger than ginger ale. "If it doesn't go away, come back in two days." Next—

This was a welcome change from the exhaustive history-taking and physical examinations of ward service. I was criticized for spending more than five minutes on my note in the chart. But after playing with a series of these absurd anagrams, I can see why the residents prefer the double crostics to be found upstairs.

July 17, 18

My final day in pediatrics. Took an "objective exam." Grades and exams are especially pointless in the third year. We had tried to talk the head of the department into abolishing them, but no luck. He kept talking about the need for an "objective standard" to place beside a personal evaluation from the staff. He had never answered my question, "Why do we need any evaluation at all?" The old doctor had met us halfway—we had to take the exam, but were given the option of signing our name to it or not.

The exam was a recap of the National Boards. The Award for Idiocy was won by the following question: At age one children are usually given shoes to (a) support the ankle, (b) encourage walking, (c) prevent internal rotation, (d) protect the feet.

Needless to say, I did not sign my name.

I don't know how my teachers will evaluate themselves on the basis of our exam answers, but I think they have done well. They had a sense of urgency about the finer details of their field—they managed to impart some of that urgency along with some of the detail. I feel that given any patient I could come up with a plan for diagnosis and treatment that would at least be acceptable even if it didn't work.

Obstetrics

July 22

First day on OB—or rather my second day. I found out I was the only student who took President Nixon at his word and observed the Man on the Moon holiday. As I suspected, the hospital got along fine without me. I am assigned to the labor room for a fortnight. Several new prerequisites. I get to wear "white pajamas," cap and mask, and shoe conductors—far superior to my usual gadget-laden short white coat and conventional shirt, tie, and pants. This is for me the ultimate in hospital fashion —it makes me look as if I *do* something. It also cuts across class boundaries—it is worn by men ranging from attending surgeons down to me.

The second advantage of the labor room is 11 free meal tickets, valued at $2 each. The limit on their use is one per day, so that I have a big lunch at the cafeteria instead of my usual 30¢ bowl of soup. I feel an obligation to use every nickel allotted to me to the extent of taking more than I can eat. I wish that the cafeteria offered things like steak or shrimp cocktail, but in the meantime will content myself with lots of meat loaf and ice cream.

After such a lunch I am tempted to take a nap in the dormitory provided for us near the labor room. Bunk beds with fresh sheets and a light blanket, paperback fiction, and a book of obstetrical cartoons. Heaven. Unfortunately for my nap, though, our afternoons are slated for antepartum (AP) clinic. My first patient was a stewardess for a Caribbean airline, eight months pregnant. This was the first time she had been in a hospital. My job was to get an obstetrical history and do a quick physical. She had filled out a questionnaire, which freed me from asking a lot of personal questions about a subject I don't really understand. Without thinking, I tried to examine her while she was sitting in a chair. This was awkward and embarrassing. Things went better with her lying down on an examining table. I was later chided for describing her breasts as "pendulous." I have a lot to learn. The resident helped me with the pelvic—i.e., he went in first and then asked me about my findings. Apart from determining the sex of the patient I did not come up with much. I resolved to review the anatomy of the region before I subjected further patients to this again. As my stewardess walked back to the dressing room I thanked her and then blushed at my mistake. "You should never thank the patient." At least not after a pelvic.

July 23

The 24 hrs of *Les Dames*. First patient was a 40-year-old black woman who practically delivered herself. The resident is a soft Egyptian who looks at every swollen abdomen as if with memories of belly dancers. He tried to attribute the trouble-free greased-lightning delivery to "excellent management," but I got him to admit that this was "the ideal woman" for the procedure: she had a "good pelvis," she had given birth twice before, and she was stoical by nature. In obstetrics, as in no other area of medicine, the patient does most of the work for you.

The resident thought it would be a good idea for me to observe the labor contractions of one patient all the way through. The nurse concurred and was glad for the company, since usually the doctors do nothing more than make hourly checks and spend their time drinking coffee in the lounge, discussing the residency programs throughout the country and reading stale news magazines; springing into action when they are told "it's on the way." I didn't mind the vigil since the nurse was pretty. The woman was having her first. Her bag of waters had ruptured prematurely and we wanted to speed things along. She pleaded for a sedative, but we needed her awake to push, and we did not want to sedate the baby along with her. Her contractions were painful, but not that strong. After dinner I asked the nurse for an estimate of the magic hour, and was told 6 AM. Very close to it; only an hour earlier. Mother was very relieved after it all! I tried to decide who would sleep the soundest —the mother, the baby girl, or me.

July 24

After a four-hour nap I showed up on AP clinic. My fatigue may have aided my charade as a doctor. Although I had gone over the anatomy of the bony pelvis, I was still "shooting in the dark" for that part of the exam. The attending suggested that I "practice" in the delivery room, after the baby had come out and while the mother was still under a regional anesthetic. Seemed like a good suggestion, so I went back up there, selected a mother of eight expecting number nine, and got the OK from the physician in charge. I had just returned from changing into my white PJ's when she was rushed in. A classmate of mine delivered the child. One, two, three, except no "four"—the baby didn't cry. I next heard the resident calling softly for a tracheal tube. The baby didn't look blue, but it wasn't breathing. A huddle of physicians worked over the child, while I stayed out of the way. The mother craned her neck; she knew something was wrong and that the baby had not cried yet. "Oh, no," she moaned. She was a religious woman: she grieved for the death of her baby, but I also detected a note of frustration. After nine months of trouble to have it come to this. "Is my baby going to die?" she asked me. I was emotionally neutral. "Pray," I said. *"Madre de Dios . . ."* Within a few seconds she was rewarded with a gurgle and cry. A true believer. The baby came around to a healthy pink, and I explored the landmarks of the bony pelvis.

July 25

On duty today and tomorrow for a total of 36 hours straight. Managed to sleep for two hours at one point, but this was just enough to give me a standard for my fatigue when I awoke. This is not only hard on me but also on my patients. I am dangerous enough at my most alert. Watched a fellow third-year student try to start an IV. Franklin is his name, and he does not "fit in" and what is more he isn't trying. Independence of spirit can be a fine thing but this experience demands a Cub Scout type of bonhommie. I was very apprehensive about this little procedure: when this guy was on pediatrics he was famous for his ineptitude at drawing blood. Instead of the usual horizontal, he would go in with a vertical approach. This time I knew he would miss and didn't want to be present for the occasion, but I figured the patient would benefit from having me there—at least I could dissuade him from trying again. Sure enough, no sooner had my colleague inserted the needle than a swelling the size of a lemon appeared on the poor lady's arm. I stopped the bleeding and walked out of the room. I am just as inept in this procedure, but I do not have his stupid, unreflecting confidence: I actually fear for my patients. I told my friend to get someone more expert to start the IV, that this lady deserved a break. Deaf ears. He told me shortly afterward that he had succeeded on the second try.

My first patient tonight was a sweet young Puerto Rican lady—six months pregnant and with a uterine infection. In pain, but otherwise at peace. I really fell for her. After many hours she finally delivered a previable fetus. I shielded the sight from her eyes, and tried to distract her with questions at this crucial moment. She acted as if she knew what was going on, but it didn't matter so long as her pains would be over. Later I asked the resident about the source of her infection. "Probably a rusty coat hanger." I had been fooled, but I was charmed by my own innocence.

Next patient was a good-natured black girl who happened to be single. This was her first child and she swore she was not going to go through it again. "From now on, I'm going to go to an adoption agency—let somebody else go through all the trouble." She had an exaggerated response to labor pains and to our "procedures"—actually I'm told most women seem unduly apprehensive the first time. "You're going to put a needle up my vagina?" she shrieked. No dear, we're going to give you an anesthetic through the back. "You mean you're going to put the needle in my back!" For all her fears, she cooperated well: I spent the night in vigil with her and got her to "push" the baby to the delivery stage—a personal triumph of the will. When she delivered, and was told that she had a little girl, she broke down: "Her father's dead in Vietnam." We were flummoxed: we had solved the most pressing problem only to learn one minute later that there was a bigger, insoluble one. Instead of the sons of Aesculapius we felt like plumbers.

July 26

After a shower at 9 AM in the "dormitory suite" I returned to work. My fatigue disappeared when I read on the board that there was a new patient who was the mother of seven. A "grand multip" (for multipara)—good news, because the residents will let third-year students deliver them under supervision. They told me to start an IV immediately—the brief history and physical could wait. Not only the multips easy to deliver but they are very "quick on the draw"—their total labor is much shorter than primips. I had selected my vein and went to get a supervisor; I had done my first successful IV earlier this AM but under expert supervision. When I returned to the room with another student I found my patient being wheeled down the hall in haste. I went to the scrub room to wash up, where I was joined by the smiling Egyptian resident. I said, "I'd like to deliver this one, sir." "I think the nurses are doing it for you." A glance at the delivery table revealed the nurses holding the baby's head which was barreling through the gates of life. I figured there was no point in me doing anything now and deferred to the resident, who disregarded his unwashed state and carried off the rest of the delivery. My grand multip had fooled me—she was too easy. Instead of magnifying my glory she proved that I was useless. I will never trust another.

July 28

Another multip. I watched her very carefully. Nice woman from Ecuador, who delivered her five previous children in her native country *"a la casa"* and refused anesthetics for this one. Slight language problem. I would come in and learn about the progress of her labor pains by inquiring "*Dolor?*" and checking her response to my interrogative thumbs up, thumbs down, or wavering hand (the last to indicate no change, but I wonder if she understood). Her labor was slow. I had just read an article in a journal about the importance of giving the patient the impression that you are relaxed and have all the time in the world to solve his problems instead of rushing from patient to patient. I practiced on this lady, pausing outside the door and entering slowly, and sitting by the side of the bed. I should have come up with some genial small talk, but my Spanish failed me. I called the lady a "*fuerte mujer*" and she declined it gracefully.

I got her to "push" the baby down, and when the wet hair of its head was just visible I got ready for the delivery. As I was dressing, the resident came in. "I'm up for this one," I told him. "Go ahead, but hurry." He guided my hands. Most babies come out with their nose to the floor, so I pushed upward to get the chin out. My next move was to free the leading shoulder, but the resident's hands were in the way. Before I could understand what was going on he had removed three coils of umbilical cord from its neck. The rest of the delivery was easy and the baby began life aggressively. I then asked the resident how he was so fast in spotting the cord complication, which could have injured the infant by cutting off his blood supply before he could breathe on his own. Turns out that if you don't always look for this you may not spot it in time. Thank God he was there. He told me I was going to get the credit for the delivery with his "assistance," but I could hardly be proud of my performance. I'd like to believe I will never miss another neck cord in my career. But I'm not so sure.

July 29

Had lunch with Eric Grey, who is distinguished from his fourth-year classmates and also from all other medical students here by the fact that he is 34 years old. He was in the public relations business, had his own firm, and had established a successful career when he chucked it for this apprenticeship. He is rumored to have brought with him the baggage of the other world—a beautiful wife, fabled apartment, and costly paintings. He is a very competent subintern, and you take him for an attending until you hear him ask the resident the same questions you were thinking of asking. Never have I come across someone who was aware of my technical problems and also expert at solving or, better yet, at guiding me toward their solution. It was he who showed me how to do my first IV. I admire him for trying to make the big jump. Had I gone into his former field I too would have grown bored with it and cast eyes at medicine, but I doubt if I could have done a sufficient public relations job for myself to bamboozle an admissions committee into taking the risk. I would have upped my drinking instead. The great thing about medical school if you are a potential alcoholic is that you just don't have time to drink. Maybe that's why he switched.

July 30

Discovered at 9 AM that I was on duty in the private OB-GYN operating room. A brief glance at my schedule also informed me that I was due there "scrubbed" at 7:50 AM. Amazed at myself (not for forgetting appointments, but for never learning to keep them) I ran up to the OR floor. The operation was in progress, so a nurse

Obstetrics

told me to wait in the "lunchroom" next door. Tried to drown my sorrows with milk and graham crackers (an ancient feature of this surgery department, I learned) and one hour later was summoned to the scrub room. The attending didn't seem to mind my tardiness at all; later when I saw how superfluous was my presence I knew why. The resident, however, was determined to save face for the department.

"Why are you late?"

"No excuse, sir."

"You realize, of course, that I will have to write a letter to the chairman of the department informing him of your absence and telling him that you seem to have a very poor attitude toward this field?"

"Fair enough."

I added, mostly for the attending's sake, that it was not deliberate, or even calculated, but negligence. Still shivering, I scrubbed in. I noticed that I managed to splash a lot of water on the tiled floor, a feat that the other two managed to avoid. The sins of negligence and sloppiness are mortal ones in this game, and I almost quit right then, to sell socks neatly and punctually.

I was the second assistant, which meant that for the most part I kept my hands not only out of the way but also on the sterile cloth draping the patient's leg where the surgeon could see them and be sure they were safely idle. I was called on to hold retractors, which is truly mindless, and to cut sutures, a job that is sufficiently difficult to be screwed up. Some sutures you want to leave with a tail of a centimeter (if they are going to be taken out later), some with a tail of 4 mm, and some with hardly any tail at all. It will be a while before I can be sure of doing this right. The resident tried to warm up, but I was still scared. He chided me for calling him "sir" (All right, sir) and for saying thank you upon being released for lunch. I would lick his bloodstained, white conducting shoes if he would forget this AM's incident. I enjoyed watching him sucking up to the attending. The operative-procedure note is a minor pain in the arse, yet he was able to tell the attending he would be "honored to write it up, sir."

Don't call him "sir."

July 31

Decided that I had to be especially conscientious for my second day in the OR. I got a list of scheduled operations last night and read the charts of all six patients, taking notes on the important points and the outstandingly trivial (e.g., one patient was "allergic" to salami). This morning I waited for a chance to show off but it was long in coming. Three simple operations went by without any discussion of the case. I was also disappointed by the fact that the patient with the thickest chart had her operation postponed because of deficient clotting factors. I had expected to confound the wise with my detailed knowledge when it came to her case. An hour last night truly wasted, because it was all for show and would never be shown.

The resident studied each chart intensively while the patient was being anesthetized. When I cruised in from lunch (on the coward's side of punctual) he put down the chart, started scrubbing and asked, "Are you familiar with the case?" This was a rhetorical question and the sentences were already assembling in his mind for the précis.

I started to scrub up. "Ask me anything." This was a hasty gauntlet, and my immediate reaction was to cover myself by qualifying "anything important, that is." But the challenge lay bare. The resident was at first astonished at my bravado and then pleased at the prospect of really nailing me to the wall. He smiled with rare sincerity, rejected several questions on the grounds that they were reasonable ones and I might conceivably get them, and then asked:

"Mrs. Budetsky had a series of blood chemistry tests done. One of the results is abnormal. Which one?"

I rinsed my hands, put on some more soap, and silently prepared a concession statement. I had memorized a few things about Mrs. Budetsky but not this. Just before surrender I remembered glancing at a table of results which were normal except for an SGOT (a liver enzyme) which was slightly elevated. This could have been in the chart of any one of the six patients, but I opted for the gamble.

"SGOT—55 International Units."

I held my breath to see how the dice landed. The resident stopped scrubbing and looked at me in amazement. "Pretty fair," he conceded. I breathed easier. Bingo.

I had missed getting nailed, but he intensified his attack.

"What are the conflicting orders in her chart?"

"You mean about the novocaine?" There was some dispute whether the patient was allergic to one of the components in this anesthetic and this could be important.

"No. On her order sheet."

Lightning did not strike twice. "I don't know."

"This patient was put on NPO [nothing by mouth] from midnight on, yet she was given oral Demerol this morning." He said this quickly to reaffirm my inferiority after the rebellion, and partly to cover up the absurdity of the question. I was glad to have lasted so long in the contest and gloated inside. The resident finished washing up and said, "You know, I think you're trying to tell me something."

You're damn right I am.

The message must have come across. After the last operation of the day he told me he was not going to report my tardiness. I told him that I deserved to get nailed for being late, but he held firm. I asked him where grand rounds were to be held and he told me. I turned to go obediently to this appointment.

"Thank you, sir."

"And don't call me 'sir'!"

Yes, sir. Hooray.

August 1

We switched to a new floor—the OB ward which gets *les girls* before and after delivery. This is my first real "ward": a big room with 12 beds, now about half filled. When you wander in wearing a white coat you are beckoned over to a bedside and told of stomach pains, or asked to change a quarter. When you go in with a syringe to draw blood, patients hold their breath till you pass.

We go on rounds with the resident and the chief attending in the morning, and otherwise we run the ward ourselves, two third-year and one fourth-year student. The resident seems my junior in a way: he is like one of those nice guys in the class below you at college whose superior competence inspires not rivalry but admiration. The "chief" is also a good guy; he is the one attending who gives me the instinctive feeling that he regularly drinks beer from the can. No pretensions. He dresses completely in white—the surgeon's costume plus the stark white coat and elegant white slip-on shoes. He is tall and of medium build, so he gives the impression of an oversize harlequin. He makes rounds with expedition; he scans the chart, asks each patient how she feels today (in Spanish if necessary), palpates the belly, checking the course of the pregnancy or the recuperation from delivery (many of our patients are postcesarean section). His great talent is his ability to leave patients alone and to teach his staff without ever lecturing to them. In criticizing your handling of the patient he says, "Ordinarily we do it this way . . ." but with an air of *tant pis* and with a shrug of the shoulders. He combines a concerned indifference about the present with precautions against the future. The wise fool.

A classmate told me he was going to quit medical school. He was a lab partner of mine all through the first year. We worked in groups of four and our group was unlucky: our two other partners had been asked to leave at the end of the first year. He had done all right so far and could be certain to graduate, but he got bored. He is on the other half of my rotation group and is now doing pediatrics. He told me he saw his career as an extension of these first two months, that he did not care to be "married to a hospital." His complaints set off sympathetic chords and I did not try to talk him out of it.

Quitting is a decision I consider daily. My day consists of 12 hours of being on my feet and under pressure, whereas my natural Aristotelian position is one of dreaming, prone. The worst part is the frustration of incompetence—your own. After this long fatiguing day you realize that you might just as well have stayed in bed, and that in some cases the patients would actually have benefited from your absence. I told my friend you have to be crazy to stay in this field, and that I was sufficiently crazy. I added that he was lucky: he had a skill—programming computers. All I could do is teach Latin. Stick it out.

August 4

A black eye and a feather in my cap. First the feather. The fourth-year student on my ward tried to tell me that in auscultating of the heart the sound of the aortic valve was heard to the left of the breastbone. I told him I remembered it as being on the right, but he persisted in his belief. This called for a friendly showdown and I went off to get my gun. I keep a handbook of physical diagnosis loaded in my black medicine bag since I own few instruments and am not allowed to stock drugs. My gun came through—the right side it was, and the fourth-year student thanked me for correcting him. I swaggered.

On rounds, though, I made a ridiculous slip of the tongue. One of our ladies didn't want any more babies and the preferred technique for sterilization is to tie both fallopian tubes—a procedure referred to as a "bilateral tubal ligation," or "BTL." I mixed it up and told the chief attending that the patient wanted a BLT.

"On dark or rye?"

"To go."

The chief grinned and shook my hand.

August 5

I had to tell one of my patients she had a venereal disease. Her newborn child had developed an inflammation around his eyes which was shown on microscopic examination to be due to gonococcus. The likeliest source was his passage through the mother's birth canal. The child was being treated; the mother was asymptomatic now, but could easily develop "pelvic inflammatory disease," which can lead to sterility or death from peritonitis. We treated her with penicillin before we got back the reports on the cervical culture—we didn't want to take any chances. But I still had to tell her.

She made it easier for me by asking, "Say, did you ever figure out what's wrong with my baby's eyes?" "As a matter of fact, we did," I replied, and went on to break the news vaguely. I felt she deserved all the tact I could muster. She was a black Jamaican and a fine lady. Nebulous phrases about an inflammation in the genital area. "You mean like gonorrhea or syphilis?" Not exactly, no, this was caused by "neisserial gonococcus" (i.e., gonorrhea). "How do you get it?" Mainly through sexual contact. "Any other way to get it?" Yes. (A lecture in bacteriology had told us it was possible to get gonorrhea on a toilet seat, but that was a hell of a place to take a date.) "I'm always very careful—I never use public rest rooms. You say it's mainly through sexual contact?" Yes, ma'am, and whoever gave it to you better get treated or you're going to get it again. "I'm just not that kind of person." It can happen to anybody. "I'm a one-man woman, and just wait till I see my husband."

During visiting hours I saw her husband come in with a bunch of roses. I tiptoed away.

August 6

When a woman on this ward is in active labor we try to get her out of the ward and into the labor room. Sometimes we miss the boat.

A friend was on duty this evening and I was working late. We got a call from one of the sick wards that a patient was in what looked like early labor. My friend went off to find the resident, and then returned to examine the woman in her bed (with the curtains drawn around it— this was visiting hours). He concluded that active labor had yet to begin—the contractions were irregular and there was no dilation of the cervix. Besides, this was her first, she would probably have a long labor. The lady's husband was there and he was worried. He had recently been in a minor car accident, and his face that of a character in the comic books who has just come out of a fight, with scrapes and Band-Aids and stitches. This guy looked tough. The resident assured the man that his wife was not in active labor, and left. My friend returned to his book on obstetrics.

In a short time another patient—a 300-lb mama who later had twins—came shuffling (yes, shuffling) down the corridor in an old red bathrobe. "You better come quick.

Mrs. Jackson says it's really hurting." My friend, since he was on duty, went down to investigate and I figured another false alarm, but realizing that soon I would be on duty, I tailed after him to learn what I could. I had never seen false labor.

When I got down to the ward the room was filled with visitors. From the bed surrounded by curtains came the unmistakable wail of someone who was too young to be in the room. I passed through the curtains to see my friend holding an infant, and the resident was sheepishly clamping the cord. I decided they didn't need me and went back through the curtains to talk to the nurse who was clearing out the visitors. There was the woman's husband, inarticulate with rage. I went up and told him everything was fine (which it was). He glowered at me and smashed his hand in his fist: he was waiting for the resident. His brother was there too, less mad and more articulate. "This was his first, but my wife has had three kids and I know there is such a thing as a delivery room. You can't let a woman do that here—there's all these people about and it's not sterile."

I agreed that this was not the ideal place, but added that these things happen sometimes (whatever justification that is) and that in this case everything was all right. A bright nurse took the husband inside the curtains to see that his wife was fine; he broke down at the reunion. Tears of joy, I hope. Later the resident apologized to him in the visitors' room, and my friend returned to his book on obstetrics.

August 7

One of my patients was a birdlike black woman who was eight or nine months pregnant—the chart was confused. Edie Feder had walked into the hospital because of a pain that "prevented her from walking." The labor room made a diagnosis of false labor and questionable separation of the symphysis,* then sent her down for us to watch. She was slim and good-looking, but tough: she was single, on welfare, with two children. A third child had died of a "head injury." May, the beautiful nurse's aide who lives on the same block, despises Edie, claiming she dropped her child and watched its head swell for three days before the neighbors finally brought it to the hospital, and by then it was too late. May hopes that Edie's present child is born dead.

Edie is a decent guest of the hospital. When she is not dozing in a chair she beckons me over with her finger and complains of chronic backaches and periodic labor pains, which are real but irregular contractions, although May and some of the other women say she is faking. She does complain about the food. "I don't see how you expect me to eat that stuff." She eats like a bird, or rather drinks, for I never saw her ingest anything more than a few swallows of orange juice. She claims she has not eaten anything solid for six weeks, "just fruit juice," and even in this area she was hard to please: she disliked our brand of orange juice and all brands of grapefruit juice and claimed she was allergic to milk and tomato juice. Bad marks also for tea anywhere and hospital coffee. She liked soda but not ginger ale (I assume that her dislike was not limited to a special brand, but I never pinned her down). I was very bored with Edie. Every day when she unloaded her food complaints on me I told her we would get the dietitian to talk to her. I asked the nurses to set up the meeting. "If she's hungry enough she'll eat" was the terse response. Good point. I don't think the dietitian ever saw her, and I looked forward to the day when Edie would attain a negative weight, rise from her bed, and float out of the window.

Nonetheless, I took a hematocrit on her, which consists

---

* The front part of the pelvis.

of pricking the finger and drawing blood in two capillary tubes, spinning these down in a desk centrifuge, and checking the proportion of red cells to serum, which is normally around 40%. In her case it was 24%; it had been 36% three days ago on admission, and the 12% drop pointed to an acute blood loss. I told the resident, who said to check it again. Again 24%. The resident was concerned and conferred with his colleagues. The consensus was a series of possibilities: (a) that my "crits" were wrong, (b) that the "crit" on admission was wrong and she was chronically anemic, (c) that both "crits" were correct and she had suffered an acute blood loss due to a hemolytic episode from a drug reaction or to internal bleeding, possibly in the womb. The last was our biggest fear, since it might come from a situation in which the placenta had been disrupted in early labor and might be disrupted further in the more forceful stages, with resulting severe hemorrhage. They decided to send her up to the labor room for close observation. Another student started an IV and I drew nine tubes of blood from her—two for immediate type and crossmatch in case we had to transfuse her, and the rest to work up her anemia. The resident complimented me on my discovery; I put on a mask of modesty and pointed out that it may turn out to be nothing at all.

I was right.

I went down to the hematology lab to see if they got the same crit as I had: theirs was 25%. Vindication. I phoned this up to the labor room, greatly relieved, and went up to see how she was doing. She was asleep, and the residents there were of the opinion that she was going to go on sleeping till daybreak—in short, there was nothing to worry about. They pointed out that I had not drawn blood for the one crucial test which would probably explain everything—a serum iron and iron-binding capacity. They had just drawn it. I went off to bed.

August 8

As the results of the tests trickled in it was like reading the last pages of a mystery novel. The tests for hemolytic anemia, including sickle cell disease and GGPD deficiency, both high on our list of suspects, were normal, and she had no antibodies against her red cells. Hemolysis was excluded, leaving internal hemorrhage and iron-deficiency anemia. Her stool was negative for blood, and she was not bleeding from the vagina; her urine was orange, but not red enough to be a route of significant loss. It was obviously going to be iron-deficiency anemia, which many pregnant women have anyway. The results came in at 4 o'clock, showing a low serum iron ($\frac{1}{2}$ normal) and a high binding capacity, clinching the diagnosis. Why hadn't I remembered that she had eaten not so much as a hot dog in six weeks? Stupido.

Controversy over how to treat her. The resident wants to give her iron injections and "load her up fast." The fourth-year student points out these are often painful and should be used only when the patient can't take iron orally, which is the therapy he recommends. We decide to give oral iron a try, and switch to the injections if we get no response. Later we got bored with Edie again, specifically with her dangerously low crit, and decided to inject iron before the oral therapy had run its course. Edie tolerated the procedure well: $\frac{1}{2}$ a gram in each buttock.

On duty tonight—very hectic, as I am responsible for five wards. A frail Spanish-speaking woman was admitted to the "problem ward." The resident examined her and diagnosed the problem as an inevitable miscarriage. Later I met three nice young men who asked after her. I had to write her up, and decided to do the physical first, since we were expecting a great change to take place soon. She was only six months pregnant, and now in great labor pains. I told her there was nothing we could do for her pains now, but that soon it would be all over. She never asked about the chances of a live birth.

I had left for three minutes to spin down a hematocrit and was walking down the hall when the nurse said, "Dr. MacNab, the patient is ready." I looked at her for clarification but there were visitors in the hall. "I'll bring you a set." It dawned on me that the moment had come. I went in to the treatment room and shut the door. Making an effort to stay calm I reassured the mother, completed the delivery, clamped the cord, and cut it. Then I told the nurse to get the resident. It was the first time I had carried out anything important on my own, and I wanted to creep back into the hierarchy fast. We both waited for the resident after the *fait accompli*. We pretended the *fait accompli* wasn't there.

Did a lot of running around that night. An expectant mother in another ward was threatening to deliver during visiting hours. I went in to examine her, a little nervously since I had to kick the husband out. I could feel that things were definitely on their way, not precipitously, but enough to justify her moving to the labor room. I wrote a brief note in her chart, sent her up, and then rushed away on another errand of mercy. Later that night, when I went up to check on her, they told me the chief resident wanted to see me. "What do you mean by describing the stations of labor in terms of fingerbreadths?" He was referring to my quick note in the chart. "Haven't you learned about the stations of labor yet?" I had, and it's a good shorthand ($+2, +1, 0, -1, -2$), but I hadn't the time then to look it up. "You'll learn more about this when you get up to the labor room." I weighed my chances of hiding the fact that I had already been up in the labor room for a fortnight. If I didn't tell him I could probably get away with it, but if he ever found out it would mean my neck (silence implies assent). Told him the truth, and his respect for my ignorance increased. (That patient finally delivered at 10 o'clock the next morning.)

I returned to the "problem ward" to write up my admitting work—on the frail lady who had miscarried, hoping to have some peace after a hectic evening. It was 1 AM. The page system, which had been silent for hours, called my name: "Dr. MacNab, Dr. John MacNab"—it never varies from the formula. I picked up the phone, dialed the page extension, and was connected with the Security Department. What now? They told me there was a naval officer coming up to see me. What now indeed. An examination of conscience revealed many sins in the past few months but none under the jurisdiction of the US Navy. From the elevator emerged an officer in summer whites whom I recognized as a college friend, a fourth-year student in another med school. After a welcome, all the warmer because of the late hour and bizarre circumstances, I stole a can of orange juice. We drank it from thimblelike medicine cups, trading stories and discussing options for careers, in the quiet hospital and dim half-light.

August 11

Another patient really made me feel stupid. Zella Rawson was 40 years old, black, the mother of three and in her fourth pregnancy. She had some third-trimester bleeding, and had been sent in for observation. She was up and around—too much so, because she was always at the nurses' station, with either a request or a complaint. The nurses disliked her and wanted us to send her home. She had been described in her chart as "manipulative"— I felt a kinship with the man who wrote that note two years ago. She complained about the tiny meals here and said she couldn't sleep because she was so hungry. She had my sympathy, and I wrote her an order for bread and butter to be given to her at night. Immediately after writing it I knew I had been manipulated. I don't know if it helped her sleep. In the course of her stay a very high blood sugar was noted. We decided to work her up for diabetes, with the glucose tolerance test (GTT). Usually the test solution is given orally, but as Mrs. Rawson had vomited it, adding that it was too sweet, in this case I had to administer it intravenously. This woman had tiny veins and I had to stick her many times, for the solution and for blood samples at various intervals afterward. I did a butcher job. I hope I never run into Mrs. Rawson in Hades. Needless to say, the test confirmed the diagnosis of diabetes mellitus. As I wrote in the orders for the trial dosage of insulin, my orders for "bread and butter, h.s. p.r.n." * mocked me. The next time a patient complains to me of hunger, I am going to sate him with 50 ml of glucose, and then administer the rest of the glucose tolerance test. Diabetes is one diagnosis I won't miss. Suspect everyone.

My mind moves to the right.

August 12

REGAN PRODUCTIONS, INC.
Proudly Presents ...
Their First Smash Hit
"A BOY IN THE FAMILY"
With the Brilliant Star
JAMES FISKE REGAN
"Hailed by critics and public as the best show this year"
WORLD PREMIERE
August 3 at 2:05 A.M.

Producer	Thomas F. Regan
Associate	Marsha Regan
Technical Advisor	Dr. Harold Oliver

* h.s. p.r.n. = hora somni, pro re nata (at bedtime, should the need arise). In diabetes mellitus the sugar in the bloodstream is high, but the sugar in the cells is low. That is why patients are hungry.

Obstetrics

DESCRIPTION OF STAR

Weight	8 lb 11 oz
Height	22 inches
Color	Delightfully Pink
Color of Hair	Dark Brown
Color of Eyes	Blue
Voice	High Tenor
Disposition	Good (Wet or Dry)

Scheduled to Run Daily
at
174 Bedford Road
WATCH FOR FUTURE REGAN PRODUCTIONS!

This is somebody's idea of wit. My one patient who was white and spoke English and who never complained, except to find out who delivered her baby (see Technical Advisor) and what was his height at birth. (This measurement is not usually released. Why not? Because then every father will want to know the height of his newborn, and the nurses have better things to do . . .) The idea is not original with the husband; it came from "another guy at the office." They press this notice upon me as a reward for my research.

Future Regan productions should also be dramatic since, like this one, they will be by cesarean section. Watch for them.

August 20

I have been out of obstetrics for a week now, and I find I miss not only the theatrics but also the succession of happy events and the relative scarcity of disease. I liked the fact that the patient was on your side and did most of the work for you. And I liked the breezy, fraternity meeting atmosphere of staff rounds, where I was surprised to note that except for a few midwives there are no women in this field. The worst thing about pediatrics was the anxiety of the parents, especially the mothers; there are many women MD's in pediatrics, and they seem to act as surrogate mothers—never letting you forget the grim urgency of the work. Things happen more precipitously in obstetrics, but the pace is smoother, and the aura of confidence is everything. I like the apparent simplicity of the field—I feel that if I spent five years at it I could become a pro. Which is a nice feeling to have, at this stage.

Obstetrics is usually coupled with another field called gynecology which is not so much fun. I expected to find it depressing. In most cases it was not, thanks to the invention of the Pap smear. Gynecologists do deal with other problems than cancer, but their field is limited in scope. For the week I spent on this service I gave this journal a bye, and tried to learn the limits of the art. At any rate, regarding the landmarks of the bony pelvis, I no longer navigate in the dark.

For the next three weeks I will be at large.

Later

My three-week vacation was highlighted by a bout of primary atypical pneumonia, caused by a bug called *Mycoplasma pneumoniae,* alias "the Eaton agent," diagnosed by my mother and the student health doctor, with confirmation by serological tests, treated at home with a course of bed rest and tetracycline, successfully and without complications. This is a form of "walking pneumonia," so it was nothing more serious than the flu, but I had to stay in bed and take my medicine. At first I didn't like being a patient, but I learned that it was easier than being a medical student and involved no loss of status. It was the best time I've had so far this year.

Orthopedics

September 15

Good morning to you.

First day on orthopedics, and the first fall that I have returned to school without buying a notebook. Unfortunately late—I asked my roommate what time they expected one to show up (this had been his previous rotation), and he told me 9 o'clock. When I walked into the small conference room on time, I was obviously an hour late; one of my classmates looked at his watch and shook his head. After finishing his discussion of the two patients whose X-rays lined the screen, the attending acknowledged my arrival with a "Good morning." Behind the 8-ball once more.

Attending is a nice guy with a sagging face who hopefully won't shaft me forever for being late today. Took us on a quick round of selected patients. One man, his leg wrapped in a cast after an auto accident, was shaving himself: he looked good after my summer of women and children. There are beds shaped like ferris wheels—used for back injuries, "helpful in getting the patient gradually to stand up." In the pediatrics division one pixielike boy tells me his chief problem is "how to keep from being bored." I ask him if the book wagon ever comes, and he replies "rarely." I will try to look after him. That looks like the chief problem in this field: long-term, enforced boredom.

We follow our attending into the operating room. A man in his middle fifties with osteoarthritis complains of pain and not being able to sit down. He has finally consented to this operation. We will work on one leg this time and do the other later. His left leg is prepped with soap, alcohol, ether, and iodine, and covered with a sticky cellophane. It now resembles a cured ham. The incision bloodies the field. Hemostasis is applied via electric cauterization: one surgeon puts a clamp on the vessel and the other "zaps" the clamp (and thus the vessel) with a lead from the machine, controlled by his foot. Very impressive. I flirt with the "circulating" nurse; with masked faces we are forced to judge each other and to talk with our eyes. She outranks me, though, and at one point had to chastise me for getting too close to the operating field. That makes her all the more attractive.

The central point of the operation is to retool the hip joint. They grind the surfaces of the ball and socket with a hemispherical drill driven by compressed nitrogen. I ask how they know when they have drilled enough. Answer: "The sound changes to a high whine." The drilling is mushy but the effect is workmanlike. Like a cross between wood and marble, also like squeezing oranges on a machine. Finally, they insert a stainless steel cup between the ball and socket and test it by moving the leg around. Simple and impressive.

In orthopedics clinic for the afternoon. One of the patients is a little girl with a lesion in her brainstem: we are following the progression of a weakness in her legs which results from this. The cause of the original lesion we do not know; it could be a tumor. The resident glances

Orthopedics

at the chart and tells me to check the movement of her foot and the length of her legs (as one is noted to be slightly shorter than the other). The mother is short and good-looking, with tear-diamonds in her eyelashes. I ask her about her daughter, if there had been any change, etc. The resident enters the booth and repeats some of my questions. All of a sudden the mother is weeping; her daughter, after a ten-second delay, follows suit. We are at a loss. Are they crying because of the girl's dim prospects? They should have hope. The resident asks the mother why she is crying. "You see, I came here at nine o'clock and they kept us waiting, and they lost her X-rays, and now it is four o'clock and I don't know why we came here." We have no ready answer.

Rounds in orthopedics are conducted in reverse: instead of a pilgrimage from patient to patient, we sit in a conference room and the patients are brought to us. One resident astounds me with his cheek. Rounds have already started when he comes in and from a table in the front picks up a news magazine, sits down, and reads it. It is like Hamlet pretending to be mad. One patient is a 12-year-old boy with one leg shorter than the other. The prolonged use of crutches has given him massive shoulders: he looks strong, and scampers around with apparent ease. He is playful, like a monkey—his chronic disability has saved him from schools. We discuss various surgical procedures. (One possibility is slowing down the bone growth in the normal leg to allow its brother to catch up.) The resident asks if there are any other recommendations for the handling of this case. I am tempted to suggest this lad be taught the art of Hephaestus, but I keep quiet.

September 16

The resident who reads magazines in rounds today concentrated on clipping his fingernails with the scissors that he uses to cut dressings. He is called upon to comment on a case and flubs a simple anatomy question about the muscles of the arm. He gives me hope. New admissions are presented. "This 32-year-old man tried to walk across the expressway last night and almost made it . . ." Orthopedics owes much to the automobile.

"A lot of people come to this clinic because they want to be loved," a resident tells me after reviewing a chart. We go into the booth to check out this woman's lower back pain. When did she first get the pain? In high school, when her parents were being divorced. Is it true that she has recently put on weight? Yes, you see there was a death in the family recently. Would she consider an operation to relieve the pain? (The acid test.) Not now, because there is a friend in another hospital who would be lost without her visits. "It seems that all the world depends on you, and that nobody cares about your pain," the resident observes. She beams at him appreciatively. I get the point. Later I call him a frustrated psychiatrist. "Not frustrated. Happy. These people want me to hold their hand, and I oblige." The witch doctor aspect of the field appeals to me, but I still hate the automobile.

September 17

On duty in the emergency room with a Japanese-American surgical intern who was fresh at this job. "Orthopedics is a good field for those who have mechanical ability, unlike me." It was an easy night, and in one of the pauses we had a discussion of Lawrence Durrell. It is unusual to meet someone in white who cares about books.

In this easy night we had

(1) A little girl, 10 years old, who was a patient in the psychiatric wards. She had tripped on a mattress and had a sore arm. What looked like a bone chip in the affected

Orthopedics

elbow turned out to be a normal ossification center when compared with films of the other elbow. In pediatric orthopedics, we are told, get X-rays of both sides.

(2) Two drivers from a head-on collision, who were led in by policemen. An elegant black girl, more shaken than anything else, and a man from the Dominican Republic with a gash on his forehead. We X-rayed their skulls. The resident asked me if I wanted to sew up the laceration. I had never sewed before, and I liked the guy. Said I would watch him this time and do the next one.

(3) A 70-year-old woman with a hazy story. She had come in Sunday night complaining of pain in her left knee after a fall. X-rays were negative, and we sent her home. She returned tonight with a "sore shoulder" on the *opposite* side. This shoulder had black and blue marks, which could have been around since Sunday. This would mean we had missed it, and she could sue us for negligence. Fortunately she was a nice old lady who just wanted to get admitted to the hospital. X-rays showed that the spheroid head of the humerus had parted company with its shaft. The diagnosis was apparent even to me. How that bone had broken in a fall on the opposite side mystified us. This woman was doubly interesting in that the other shoulder point had "fibrosed"—it was now a mere "attachment." The resident asked me how I would treat this lady. I replied that I would "reduce" (reset) the broken humerus and put that shoulder in a cast for three months. "Now tell me," my interrogator went on, "why that is the wrong thing to do." Making an about-face, I fished for "contraindications." There is no integrity at this stage of the game—just say what your superior wants to hear. The "right" answer is as follows: this is an old lady, with a broken right arm and a fibrotic left shoulder. To put her right shoulder in a cast would leave her with no functional shoulder joint for six months. Furthermore, when the cast came off, she would have a "frozen shoulder." This stiffness can be overcome by

"working it out," but this patient would be too old to try, and her shoulder would remain frozen for the duration. Instead, they would set the arm as best they could and keep it in a sling for three weeks. Then, when the mend was "sticky," they would put this patient through intensive physical therapy, to loosen up the joint. Not an ideal repair, but this was hardly an ideal candidate.

We were trying to decide whether she would have to be admitted or whether we could treat her and send her home. Did she live alone or does somebody live with her? "Alone." Did anyone bring her here? "No, I came in an ambulance." When was the last time she had gone to the bathroom? "This afternoon." Had anyone helped her? "Yes, my maid." Raised eyebrows and disbelief. What was her maid's name? A name, address, and phone number were provided, which were verified by the telephone directory. The maid wasn't in, so the old lady was admitted. She was very pleased.

At 11 o'clock, I left my phone number and called it a night.

September 18

I got turkeyed twice today by the same anatomical unit. We were watching a "total hip replacement" from the gallery. In this operation both ball and socket of the joint are replaced by prostheses. One of the residents had spent last year in England with the man who had "invented" the operation, and now he was showing the attending surgeon, his superior, how it was done. This required tact. We couldn't hear through the glass, but I could see the resident demonstrating techniques and imagined him saying, "In England they find it easier to do it this way, sir." It was good to see the art being transmitted in the different direction, from younger to older for a change.

The regular direction was resumed. As we watched, our

Orthopedics

preceptor quizzed us. "What structure lies posterior to the joint, MacNab, that would be a source of concern during an operation?" I was ignorant and silent. "The sciatic nerve," responded one of my classmates. "Is your name MacNab?" I should not have missed this.

Later, in clinic, we examined a patient who had a jagged scar down one buttock and onto the back of her thigh. "What structure does that make you think of?" an attending asked me. "The sciatic nerve," answered another of my colleagues. I missed it again. Somebody had told me that if they asked me any questions during my stint in the private GYN operating room, a good answer was always "the ureter" (this was the right answer twice in fact). I will never forget the key to orthopedics.

September 19

We had another sciatic nerve question and this time I got it. I am slow but stupid. We were watching an operation for straightening a deformity of the back called scoliosis—a hump on one side of the back. Very disfiguring. It usually occurs in girls and is usually "idiopathic" in origin, which means "we dunno." A good research project for a lifetime, even if it didn't pan out. This case was a 14-year-old girl, and her vertebrae were exposed to resemble those of an uncooked chicken. After an hour of scraping muscle away from bone, two 8-inch steel shafts were locked onto either side of her spine. Bone chips were taken from the rear of her hip and placed in between the central vertebrae, to fuse them in their locked alignment. In a year the steel rods will be removed. This operation provides "not a total correction," our preceptor told us, "but it's a big improvement." To the spectator it seems that the surgeons are trying to destroy the patient and succeeding.

September 20

One of the surgeons brought to clinic today a new toy. It resembled a Steinberg corkscrew and is designed for use in the repair of the anterior cruciate ligament of the knee. (Many surgeons believe that this ligament is not worth repairing, except perhaps in the knee of a professional athlete.) The residents crowded around and we went through the instruction manual, which taught the essentials of this procedure with 15 captioned pictures. We took turns playing with it. Orthopedics has the most gadgets.

September 22

Got another two "sciatic nerve" questions today. I can't miss. One preceptor is pleased by the alacrity of my response.

Diagnosed a ganglion this afternoon—a "bump" on the wrist which is a cyst of special joint cells. No *coup*, as these things are common, but it was fun to apply knowledge I had picked up 20 minutes before.

Saw a boy whose set of distal extremities at birth consisted of one webbed hand and the rest stumps. After many operations he can walk without crutches and untie his shoelaces. He seemed happy enough. He carried a textbook on French literature, and I warned him about the frustrations of that course. "Have you ever taken it?" he asked me. "Several times," I said. He told me he enjoyed the subject. Nature has blessed him with the capacity to make the best of things.

At rounds, in a discussion of procedures in foot surgery, one doctor said that a particular operation was best if you wanted to "dance and play tennis."

In pediatrics, health is freedom from bad kidneys; in

GYN it is freedom from cervical cancer. In orthopedics, health is the ability to "dance and play tennis." Not always, of course—there are patients like that boy in whom ambulation is a triumph—but often enough to be true. Remember, strong active people are good people. The country-club theory of health.

September 23

I watched the civilized intern in the emergency room try to "reduce" a dislocated thumb on a kid who had been trying to catch a football (street game). The intern had trouble with anesthetizing the nerves via a shoulder injection, and after much painful probing he delivered the drug through the thumb joint. Anesthesia not sufficient, his attempt to yank the thumb back was excruciating and a failure. The resident, who was giving him a chance to learn, finally stepped in and did it right in four seconds. The kid, who had been man enough not to cry, taunted us with a disgusted "rookie doctors." "What did you say?" asked the resident, bending the thumb again. The kid took back his statement.

The resident is a funny guy whom some liken to Jonathan Winters. I think Art Buchwald is closer to it, minus the cigar of course. He started talking on the subject of what it takes to be an emergency room physician. He says you have to be decisive, that it is better to act on the chance that yours may be a wrong diagnosis than to do nothing at all. This is the opposite of what we have been taught in the rest of the hospital: if you are not completely sure of what you are doing, then it is best to do nothing. The resident admitted that his policy had some drawbacks; it could kill people. He told me about the two people he had killed. Both old and both emergency room situations—so it goes. I envied him his candor and his self-confidence.

September 24

We were taken around to see various forms of traction. One middle-aged lady was recovering from a God-awful collision which occurred nearly two weeks ago. She had broken her femur; her traction was conventional.

"Weren't you involved in that accident on the bridge?" asked the tall resident.

"Yes, two weeks ago Thursday."

"I think I saw your car on the bridge the next day. It didn't look as if it were worth very much."

"To hell with the car—I lost my husband. You can always replace the car."

Our group said thank you and moved on to the next patient.

We had an exam in orthopedics today. We were told not to worry about it so I worried plenty. Last night I tried to memorize the operations indicated for each of the several congenital abnormalities of the hip, but gave up. I could not keep the deformities straight, let alone the surgery. I had checked the reserve text on orthopedics out of the library overnight and tried to blitz it during breakfast. My roommate, who took this course in August, asked me some "easy" questions. I flubbed them. Put my hope in the theory of predestination: nothing, not even my sophisticated ignorance, would keep me from passing that course. Everybody passed, usually.

Our preceptor grilled us in the morning session, still maintaining that we should not worry about the exam. I found that, unlike previous sessions, this time I knew some of the answers. The value of fear. Finally the attending asked what is the first thing to do at the roadside for a victim of a bad accident. This I knew, because I had missed it at breakfast (then I had said, "Stop the bleeding," and that answer is wrong).

I alone raised my hand. The preceptor called on me,

certain that I wouldn't know. (It would be not uncharacteristic.)

"First make sure the airway is patent and insure adequate ventilation. Then stop the bleeding."

"You hit the nail on the head!" He was pleased. "I see somebody has got to you already about this." (Obviously I would never deduce this answer on my own.)

The exam itself was a snap. Almost all of the questions had been covered in our session this morning. The car accident was there, and there was a question that demanded, "Why, the sciatic nerve!" in response. I missed a question on Sprengel's deformity, which was mentioned this morning. I wanted to guess that it was a congenital elevation of the scapula, but I knew that if it were wrong I would look like a fool. Turns out my hunch was right, but in medicine we are told not to play hunches and not to guess. The satisfaction of sticking to the principle was pale beside the remorse of seeing the long-shot I would have bet on win.

Spent the afternoon putting plaster casts on each other and cutting them off. Innocent fun—like playing with mud pies. Goodbye orthopedics.

Urology

September 25

Introduction to urology. We meet in the department's library, furnished in the style of a men's club. The rotarian preceptor spends time showing us the tools of his specialty; he really is like a salesman showing his "line." Later an emeritus urologist comes in, in appearance and character the last of the snake-oil vendors. He demonstrates the automatic projector and reels of color movies of operations—a demonstration done with facility and with pride. Step right up.

Later we are shown the department's own X-ray machines and electron microscope. The showpiece is a room filled with equipment to study the mechanics of urination. Even the sound is studied—and by something which used to be called a "Pitter-Patter." Our preceptor salesman thinks his own invention of a miniature FM transmitter which floats inside the bladder is more useful. Who knows? He may be right.

September 26

We go on rounds at a nearby city hospital associated with the medical center. Room after room filled with middle-aged men with neoplasms of the GU (genitourinary) tract. I get bored after the first five or so, but we keep going. Unwillingly, I am impressed with the frequency of cancer in this area. The old men look at us with dread as we approach them. Their wards are much more depressing than their equivalents in gynecology.

Our attending is a creation of Sinclair Lewis—a booster, a man with a belief in "this great land of ours" and confidence in "what the future may bring." I figured out the connection between urology and snake oil. Prostatic neoplasia is seen frequently. Most of these tumors are dependent on androgen hormones, and one of the methods of treatment is the surgical removal of the testicles. Anyone who has to convince a patient that castration will be good for him has got to be able to sell snake oil, and keep it moving fast.

September 27

Spent this fair day attending a course on hypnotism which will last for 7 Saturdays. Small auditorium filled with psychiatrists and such who pay $25 per session. I get in free, but appreciate it more because it has a price. Taught by a psychiatrist who believes the trance state is a form of hyperconcentration rather than of sleep. The man is like a laser beam—coordinated, focused energy, with no static, seen or unseen. He makes no claims for his approach other than that it is simple and effective, and a whole lot easier than the "You are getting sleepy" method.

The mechanics of his technique: have the patient look

up without moving his head. The farther back he can roll his eyes, the better a candidate he is for hypnosis. Then have him close his eyelids with his gaze fixed overhead. A patient whose eyeballs race downward before the advancing lids will be a difficult subject. (The worst subject is the one who, when asked to look upward, stares you straight in the face.) Bonus points for squinting inward in the overhead gaze. These signs are empirical correlations with the ability to be hypnotized. The lecturer said they may have something to do with the fact that alpha rhythms on the EEG are associated with periods of concentration, that rapid eye movements (REM's) during sleep are associated with dreams and with alpha rhythms on the EEG. I like this suggestion.

The lecturer induces his subjects by having them look up and then close their eyes. Two skeptical volunteers from the audience were soon hypnotized and told their left arms were buoyant. Released from the trance but not from the suggestion, they look ridiculous as they answer our questions, sitting there with left arms floating in midair. Stooges? It is possible but not probable.

The main act is a subject he has worked with before, around 40 years old, and now in the trance "regressed" to his tenth birthday, his fourth birthday, and ultimately to the age of 2 months. If this is acting it is very convincing. At 2 months he has a grasp, suck, and weak rooting reflex; he ignores a match lit 6 inches away from his face. At 4 years his eyes are open; he counts up to 7 on request but fails with the alphabet. When the hypnotist takes out a match the subject tells him that he is not supposed to play with them. At 10 when asked if he can recite the alphabet he says, "Of course, what a stupid question." He now instinctively blows out a lit match. When he comes out of the trance he remembers nothing of what went before, which the audience will never forget. Your respect for human ingenuity goes up, for human dignity down.

September 29

Every morning we are on the floor by 7:45 to learn to read urological X-rays. We are led by a friendly junior resident who is not too distant from our own position of ignorance. Urology is satisfying in that it allows you to "trace the wires." If you have a question about the interpretation of a radiograph there is always a further step to take which should give you your answer.

I am assigned a patient to "follow"—for the first time this does not involve any work. Mitch Feldman is charming and he is 91 and short. His glasses are owl-sized with thick black frames; he conceals the bald dome of his head by combing the long hair at the back of his skull forward (it is long enough to get in his eyes). He looks like a cross between Mr. Magoo and a baby sparrow that has just escaped drowning.

He has two main problems—a lesion in his left kidney that may be cancerous and one in his prostate that definitely is. As the junior resident said (in his presence), he poses "interesting medical and philosophical questions." He is 91, and anemic, but his mother lived to 102 and he looks as if he could easily surpass her. We decided that because kidney tumors are slow-growing, we will ignore the lesion in the kidney, whatever it is. (We saw a funny area on the X-ray intravenous pyelogram; we could work it up further, but the procedure would be too risky in this case.) Therefore we are sending him to a rest home for a month, to counteract his anemia and bring his hematocrit up to a point where we can treat the prostatic neoplasia by surgery or radiation. Mitch tells the chief resident that he's "leaving it up to you, doctor. Whatever you say." He is an inspiration.

We spent the afternoon in the soft leather chairs of the library drinking Cokes provided by the department and listening to one of the attendings tell us about his research. He discovered how to tell the difference between a Wilms' tumor and a neuroblastoma of the kidney—an important diagnosis to make, as the first usually disappears after drug treatment and the second demands radical surgery. He said that his technique had saved a girl (who had been misdiagnosed) from the mutilation of being chopped in half and that that "made it all worthwhile." Nolo contendere. He warned us about his tendency to go off on tangents, and then went off on a long tangent about DDT and the shells of birds' eggs. He finished up with an account of his latest project, which is the discovery in prostatic neoplasms of a viruslike particle which can cause cancer in the prostate of rats. This is big news, but if he had not told us it might be five years before I learned it. A pleasant afternoon and interesting problem.

September 30

One of the important requirements for being a doctor is to have an artillery of euphemisms, especially when making rounds. When you want to indicate that the patient four feet away is stupid, you say that he is blessed with "cerebral cytopenia"; you say that there was a "profusion of hemoglobin" to indicate his operation was a bloody one. On rounds today, a resident said that the patient around whose bed we gathered had been found to have "a stage C mitosis" of the bladder.

"You mean cancer" said a third-year student (Franklin).

I could not believe his insensitivity, and tried to throw the veil of confusion into the discussion. "No, neoplasia"—injecting another euphemism. "I'll explain it to you later." I am not against telling patients the truth, but they should not have it broken to them on rounds.

The head of the department gave us a welcoming talk

Urology

with some practical advice. He outlined the requirements for certification by the American Board of Urology and stressed the importance of being "board certified in whatever field one went into.* "The requirements are so easy that it's silly not to." One important consideration was time—most surgical specialties demand a five-year residency, and then there is a two-year Armed Forces commitment which is inescapable. He outlined our options in the area of military service and discussed each in terms of our nonmilitary careers. This was the first time that anyone had bothered to talk to us on the subject, and we were grateful. He ended with an injunction to "respect the patient's comfort in all urological procedures, including cystoscopy, catheterization, and rectal examination. The patient assumes that if you are careful in small matters, you will be in large ones, and vice versa." He is very successful.

October 1

Today I am 25. Am I happy with what I am doing? Actually, ma'am, I would prefer to be motorcycling full time. Toward Mexico.

A bottle of 1896 port was opened for the occasion. Memorable.

---

* To be certified as a specialist by the American Board of _____ (the pertinent specialty) means that the physician has done several years' residency in his particular field and has passed a difficult examination. Many states allow doctors to call themselves specialists after their internship, and these charlatans are to be avoided (quiz the secretary or look for his Board certificate on the wall). This advice comes to you free of charge—well, almost.

October 2

We had a cozy talk on sex from one of the attendings. He told us this was "a very sensitive area" and that patients were often ashamed of their problems. An old doctor he knew used to start the interview by taking a $5 bill from his wallet, laying it on the desk, and telling the patient, "This is yours if you tell me something I haven't heard before." Our attending pointed out that doctors as a rule know less about sex than any other profession does. "You boys generally enjoy your work and are too busy, too poor, or too tired to experiment." He urged us to be able to advise patients in this area. "Remember, it's the world's greatest indoor sport."

I was on duty at the chemistry lab for the third night this week. (Bertolt Brecht is right about economics.) At 11:58, two minutes before quitting time, the phone rings and a harried resident asks me if I can do a set of electrolytes, a CBC (complete blood count), and a type and crossmatch for a blood transfusion. He tells me that he has just received a patient from another hospital, bleeding after an incomplete abortion. He was highly annoyed at the bureaucratic mismanagement of this patient—she should not have been transferred in this condition. I told him that I could do only the chemistry tests, and that this official procedure requires my supervisor's consent for work done after midnight because it involves overtime. I was very tired and wanted to go home to sleep, but I realized this was a true emergency, and I offered to do the tests without calling my supervisor if he would let me take a shortcut which would save me an hour. "No, sir," he said righteously, "I want you to call your boss. I want to raise as big a stink as possible about this admission." I wanted to sleep so much that I did not have the heart to call my boss. I did the tests. They took a long time sending me the blood, and I decided not to rely on the quick qualitative procedure (although its result was verified by the longer quantitative one). I turned in the results at 3 AM to the resident who was scrubbing for the operating room. He was calmer now; he thanked me and told me he appreciated it. I felt glad I was not in his shoes—not yet.

October 3

I dreaded going on those endless rounds at that city hospital again today, but I felt that our attending would be insulted and annoyed if too many third-year students cut today. I walked around like a zombie, still drugged from last night, and fought to remain vertical. Again patients, symptoms, and surgical procedures were blended in my mind. Toward the end, I decided to experiment with a trance state to see if it could help my concentration. I followed the procedure for a self-induced trance, and found I was able to imagine the outline of a man, simplified as in a television commercial, while the resident presented the 34th case. My eyes were open but not focused.

"This 62-year-old man . . ."

I set the number 62 on the forehead of my cartoon.

"Came in complaining of urinary retention and low back pain."

I gave him an overflowing bladder and had rays pulse from his sacroiliac.

"Physical examination revealed a 40-gram prostate without nodularities."

I placed the prostate around the neck of the bladder, and affixed the correct numeral for its weight. There were now two organs in the cartoon.

"Serum acid phosphatase was normal."

This enzyme test is usually elevated in prostatic carcinoma. I decided on a color code for relevant blood tests:

blue for normal, red for elevated, green for low. The possibilities for shadings are attractive. I colored my man blue.

Imagining the X-rays and surgery was easy. When the resident finished, the picture was complete in my mind. For once I understood the key features of a case that had not been my responsibility. They could have asked me anything.

Went to dinner at a friend's house—mostly medical students, one of whom was also taking the hypnotism course. We graded the others on their hypnotizability, using the eye test. All "threes" and "fours," potentially hypnotizable. After dessert the sister of my hostess, a shy, pretty girl, said, "You haven't graded me." I looked in her eyes and I knew she was all mine. She turned out to be a four. "Would you like me to try to hypnotize you?" Shy giggles and an "I guess so," with a "what am I getting myself into" look. I took her into the kitchen, sat her down, and began the procedure. I had to start her hand up, but it continued after I released it. I kept talking; it was like surfing in the curl of a wave—you have to keep going or you are lost. When I had her open her eyes, her hand was still up there and she said she didn't feel she could bring it down. I was satisfied and released her. I had a tremendous sense of exhilaration or enthusiasm in its original sense: I felt that it was not me, but a god within me who pulled it off. My subject, whether in response to my command or not, found the whole thing amusing. She said she had been hypnotized once before, as a little girl, and had been interested enough in Zen to practice concentration exercises. My hostess was annoyed at me for fooling around with her sister, who, it turned out, had just finished psychotherapy. She is probably justified in her annoyance, but I knew I couldn't miss.

October 6

The urology department is *very* interested in persuading some of us to go into urology. It is like being rushed for a college fraternity. Generally the younger men do the "rushing." They are down on internal medicine, and see a kind of intellectual masturbation in its abstruseness.

"In medicine," a fine young resident told us, "they would be worried about this patient's stool helium. We are only trying to free him from living on a toilet seat." (The patient had urinary incontinence.) "We realize that urology does not have much prestige in medical school, but generally the less prestige a specialty has the more it can do for the patient's life."

I spent this evening typing up my urology paper, required of all third-year students. It was titled "Problems in Male Fertility: The Semen Examination and the Use of the Split Ejaculate" (I am tempted to append it for prurient interest). The typing took me an hour a page. I realize why I went into medicine instead of law school or graduate school: I can't type. Fortunately this paper is the last one I shall ever be assigned to turn out; from now on I will be writing for fame or fortune instead of a letter grade. Goodbye hack work.

October 7

It was arranged that we practice rectal examinations. Some patients with "interesting prostates" were found and talked into "having some doctors check them over." "Almost done, Mr. Jones, just two more doctors." Franklin (who plans a career in neurological research) goes in too roughly, and Mr. Jones cries out as those oh-so-sensitive nerve endings are activated and fire. My sympathies are with Mr. Jones instead of knowledge, and I pass up the chance to join in on this combination gang bang and butt fuck.

We had a lecture this afternoon on lower urinary tract infections and discussed the differential diagnosis of the penile drip. The kid was a star. (I am the kid.) The lecturer was the real star, though. This attending was the personification of the American Army in the Far East. Definitely American: stocky, cattle breeder build, flattered by a torso-hugging electric blue suit; plain-talking Great Plains accent, and GI brush cut. For the Oriental aspect I can offer only the globed head with a hint of the East in the curved eyebrows, the Japanese silk tie flashing a fiery dragon, and a range of experience with this subject that only an occupation army can provide. To ignite his cigarette he uses a gold-plated lighter in the shape of an automatic pistol, which he carries around in his trousers pocket. Yes.

Anesthesiology

October 8

Our attending, like a shoe salesman, gives us an introductory lecture on the history of selling shoes. He points out that all the early anesthetic agents were known to be anesthetic agents many years before they were used this way. Pain is no longer felt to be heaven-sent.

He has an "anesthesia cart" for us to play with. I try breathing straight oxygen for a while. Since I was not tired or hung over, I could not really attest to its reputed invigorating effect. Inhaling nitrous oxide, or "laughing gas," is like drinking very good scotch: it goes down smoothly, without burning. Within 20 seconds you reach the state my family calls "clinically drunk," in which you realize you better sit down and you better not drive home. You come out of it fast, though, too.

October 9

I am assigned to the anesthesiology branch of the eye service. This is a very easy rotation: we start at 10 instead of the usual 7:30. The attending lets me handle my first patient, a child who had to be anesthetized for an eye examination.

"Think, now, what agent are you going to use for the induction?"

"Nitrous oxide, sir," I replied, remembering my experiments of yesterday.

"Fine. How much are you going to use?"

I set the dials, remembered to include oxygen in my mixture, and set the mask over the patient's face. The others held his arms. Slowly, the child went limp—a miracle. The examination over, the attending turned off the gas and carried him to a crib. Slowly, the child woke up. Another miracle.

Had a full-scale operation to handle under supervision. The patient was a young girl who was going to undergo surgical correction of her eye muscles. Nothing too serious. "Remember, if they lose a patient during an eye operation, it's the anesthetist's fault." The little girl was very cooperative. Seconal premedication had failed to make her sleepy, but she was not afraid. "The worst thing you can do to these kids is to force the anesthesia upon them. They remember that fight all their lives." We didn't have to force it on her; she held the mask just above her face, while we kept our hands off. After a minute or so she was very tired, so we held it for her. Soon she was "deep" enough to try to "intubate" her—tracheoscope her, put down an endotracheal tube. "Go ahead now." I had practiced on a rubber dummy yesterday, but this was a real little girl—slightly more difficult.

"What do you see?" asked the attending after 15 seconds of my fumbling.

"Going through the tonsils now, sir."

"Tonsils, hell, you should be at the epiglottis by now." He was right, I should have. I fumbled around for two seconds more, but then realized my patient was unable to breathe as I experimented and thrust the instruments into the hands of the pro.

"The first day you're all fingers."

Thumbs.

October 10

I was given another patient to handle, and did much better. A small boy who was going to have an eye removed because of a tumor growing inside it. He was a Norman Rockwell boy, but the case was not maudlin: he would live and glass eyes can look very realistic (I went out with a girl off and on for a year before I learned the truth behind her occasional "cross-eyedness"). The boy was easy to handle and easy to intubate.

"Are you in?" the attending asked me.

"I think so, sir."

The attending squeezed the rubber bladder and we watched the patient's chest rise in response. "What do you know, you are in."

I felt a little embarrassed that I had been able to "master" the essential procedure of this specialty so early.

In the operating room there are two main subgroups. The anesthesiologist can talk with his assistant, but otherwise communicates only with the patient in a one-way conversation, listening to his heartbeat, blood pressure, and respirations, and recording these figures at five-minute intervals. The operating team ignores the patient, and concentrates on an anatomical region. There is usually a conversation between the operator and his assistant which often includes the operating nurse, but never the anesthetist. I listened.

The surgeon was a youngish man who resembled Woody Allen and now is trying to enjoy the adolescence he lost out on because he looked like Woody Allen. He tried to cajole the nurse (a terrifying matron) into coming along with him to an ophthalmological convention in another city.

"Take your wife," the matron clucked reprovingly.

"Any man who goes to a convention and shacks up with his wife has got to be a queer."

We all felt differently, but the ribaldry stood safe from criticism because he was the high priest.

He got to talking about tomorrow's football games with the enthusiasm peculiar to those who were too light to play football. (An ex-water boy? I don't think so.) He mentioned he had a $50 bet on one of them. I wondered what fraction that was of the fee he was going to charge for his morning's work, and what $50 represented to the boy's parents. I doubt they had a bet on the game.

October 11

This meeting of the hypnotism course was a "bread and butter" session. The audience is now acquainted with the technique of hypnosis; we were now told how to apply it. The essence of the lecture:

(1) For psychoanalysis: leave this to the psychiatrists.

(2) For pain relief: don't say, "You will no longer feel the pain," because a patient of no more than ordinary suggestibility will still feel it and you will have "blown your cool." Tell him instead that the sensation will be "filtered through a blanket of numbness." The ideal response: "The pain is still there, but it doesn't hurt." (Supposedly the response after morphine.) Also, teach the patient self-hypnosis, so his pain control is self-sufficient.

(3) For changing habits, especially for stopping smoking: mention of the word "cancer" is superfluous. Instead, have the patient concentrate on the allegiance he owes to his body, as for a babe on the doorstep. Again, teach him

self-hypnosis, so that this matter is his alone, and not between you and him.

Graduates of the last two applications came in to answer questions. They were intelligent and had a dignity that the most suggestible patients often lack. In the afternoon an obstetrician told us about the use of hypnosis in his own specialty. He showed us a movie of himself doing a cesarean section on a patient whose anesthesia consisted solely of a hypnotic trance. He addressed her steadily during the operation, and she sang softly. Very impressive. He told us he always gives his patients a choice of anesthetics. Hypnosis is especially useful in obstetrics because conventional anesthetics can depress the baby and decrease the mother's pushing (which is usually safer than a doctor's pulling). Another point: gases often induce vomiting, which can lead to aspiration, and the ladies usually come in at night, with a stomach full of supper.

So far I have met nobody in the anesthesiology department here who knows or cares about hypnosis. It is fair to say they would have little use for it in their service to this metropolitan hospital. In obstetrics, for example, many of the ward patients have not seen any doctor in the course of the pregnancy, let alone the doctor who will deliver them. (The obstetrician who lectured us would "induce" his consenting patients starting with their first antepartum visit.) Hypnosis in obstetrics is a personal thing, and most hospitals rely on assembly-line procedures. Still, there is a place for hypnosis in the anesthesiologist's bag of tricks, along with the tank of nitrous oxide and the open can of ether.

October 13

I was chastised for my hubris of thinking I had mastered the technique of intubation. Working on a pubescent girl,

I put the tube down the wrong hole (it was placed in the esophagus instead of the trachea). The resident stepped in and did the job right, consoling me with the fact that he got his first one and missed the next four. This is a trick that I would really like to be able to do right every time.

The surgeon today asked his assistant when the residents would like to come out for a spin in his yacht.

"The end of the month looks good. Some of the fellows asked if we could take our wives along."

"That might be a bit difficult. It's not a very big boat."

"Well, then, maybe you could cut it down to whoever really wants to come."

"Yes, that's possible."

"This is a very nice tradition of yours, sir."

"Yes, thank you. I am surprised that more attendings don't do it. Much more common in my day."

"This time I think I'll really get something out of it. I took sailing lessons this summer."

You see, O resident with beads of perspiration above your mask, that familiarity with the pastimes of the rich can be as important to your career as a knowledge of the neuroanatomy of the pupillary reflex. Sail on—but first, you must learn not to sweat.

October 14

The patient scheduled for removal of a cataract was an 86-year-old woman with a restless movement of her toothless jaw and nearly unintelligible speech. I wondered whether her age and condition made the operation justifiable, but decided that restoration of sight (she was blind in the other eye) would make anyone's life livable, however it seemed before. She also had a sense of humor.

"Is this the operating room?"

No, this is where we put you to sleep.

"Oh, the gas chamber." She cackled, and we laughed too.

It was an uneventful operation. We monitored the patient's EKG on an oscilloscope, and there were no surprises (although an arrhythmia would have been no surprise). When the surgeons left, though, we could not get the patient to breathe on her own. (This normally recurs in a few minutes.) This apnea was no emergency—we continued to ventilate her with the rubber bag, but this could go on for two days and we wanted to go to lunch. The attending anesthesiologist came in, studied the patient, and suggested that the short-acting muscle relaxant was sticking around longer than it should, paralyzing her respiratory muscles. We gave her another five minutes with no change, and then injected an antagonist to the first drug. She started breathing gradually, and we went off to lunch.

Not all drugs, however, have antagonists.

Because there were no cases scheduled, I got the afternoon off, with the recommendation that it be spent in the library. Instead I watched the World Series at a local tavern with a color TV and a 20¢ draft. The oldest form of anesthesia. Medicine has some long days, but this was not one of them.

October 15

I submitted my application for an elective abroad in my fourth year. Of the hospitals offered my choices were for ones in Thailand, Korea, and Colombia. I don't really care where I go, but I would like to spend some time in a foreign country with a crying need for doctors (I realize there is a similar need in our own country, but there are laws here which keep fourth-year students from playing Albert Schweitzer). This elective is one of the few things I am looking forward to.

I showed up in my assigned operating suite to discover that the only case requiring general anesthesia had already been done. I eschewed the library and also the World Series to participate in the Moratorium for Peace. I had never taken part in a demonstration before. In college I had no sympathy for any causes, and previously in medical school I was too scared—I felt that my marginal level scholarship could not afford time out for anything but work or entertainment. (This year my level of scholarship has dropped from marginal to nil.) I thought I could avoid complicated issues like politics by going into medicine, but this is no longer so. Still, even today my loyalties were divided. How would one of my patients feel about being put to sleep by a pseudo-doctor with a black armband *in addition* to his need for a haircut? I felt it best not to provoke needless anxiety and waited until I left the hospital to put on that badge. Could I now afford to take off to demonstrate? I am glad that it was an easy day and I did not have to make that choice. I learn very little in a given day, but seven such days may be the sum of my preparation in anesthesiology in my medical career. If there had been a case scheduled, I would have stayed to work on it. I was sorry to have to leave the demonstration for a four o'clock lecture and my job, but again there was no real decision. The lecture was on "cardiac arrest," i.e., what to do when the heart stops pumping, and my evening job later entails doing emergency blood chemistries. At midnight, when I was free, the day of Moratorium was over, and I went to bed.

October 16

I was assigned to the open-heart room for the day. An old man with a calcified aortic valve was to have a mechanical valve inserted. He was a nice man, definitely worth the risk of an operation in spite of his 70 years, and I wished him luck as he went under.

The surgeons began this heart operation by working on the right leg, to insert catheters for venous and arterial pressure. These men have the most glamorous role in medicine, and one is struck by their "ordinariness"—instead of being uncommon men they seem downright common. They do have a kind of patient directness that I have not found anywhere else. They pride themselves on their virility, and probably think of other doctors as a bunch of old ladies. I thought they would be the priests, but they are the hunters of the tribe.

"In this business," one of them said to the other, "if you have to be either smart or lucky, it's better to be lucky."

One amusing thing: they had a tape deck system in the operating room which emitted the kind of music you hear in supermarkets. Just as they hooked up "the pump"—the heart-lung machine—a player-piano version of "Pennies from Heaven" came on in perfectly synchronized rhythm, making the pump seem like a Rube Goldbergian musical instrument. Actually, it is very hard to adjust your thinking when working with this machine. I asked the anesthesiologist why he had stopped ventilating the patient with the rubber bag. Was it because the surgeons wanted the chest to be still? He said yes, and pointed out that there was no need for the patient to breathe, as the pump was bubbling oxygen through his blood. I felt like a farmer.

The old valve was obstructed with calcifications—the X-ray had not lied. They reamed these out and set the new valve into place, a ball in a cage type of affair. It looked as if it would work. I did not stay around to watch the end of the operation because the tape deck was starting on its fourth time around, and I could stand it no more.

October 17

"Cardiac arrest—stat—fourth floor" was the message from the omnipresent loudspeaker. "You might as well go," said the anesthetist for pediatric surgery. "They're going to be late in sending up our patient."

Cardiac arrests are not to be used as teaching exercises—that is the hospital policy. I felt that I might be useful (it was 7:30 in the morning) or else would keep out of the way.

The curtains were drawn around one bed where a half-dozen residents and interns tried to resuscitate a heavy-set older man, breathing for him by squeezing a rubber bag, pumping his chest, starting IV's, feeling for pulses, monitoring his bizarre EKG, and once or twice "zapping" him with the defibrillator. The man was gray, and his massive flesh was cold and damp. He looked like death not even warmed over. By comparison the young doctors looked like fashion mannequins with their white suits and jazzy ties—the take-charge generation. The old man rallied his powers and tried to free himself from his rescuers.

It was as if they were trying to kill him.

"I think he's trying to tell us something," one resident mused. But it was only a thought, and they continued the therapy. I heard later that resuscitation efforts were unsuccessful.

Pediatric surgery was good to get back to. I had met this surgeon when I was on pediatrics (the case of the misplaced femoral catheter) and the assistant on orthopedics (the civilized Japanese intern, now making his first hesitant slice). The operation was used as a teaching experience; the surgeon lectured as he cut or advised when the younger man had the scalpel. Two first-rate people.

The anesthetist talked about his plans to (1) finish his residency in anesthesiology, (2) complete a residency in internal medicine, and (3) go to law school at night and become an expert in medical law (or was it legal medicine?). I was impressed. I knew that anesthesiology was dull, but had not realized its boredom could spawn such Titanic ambitions. I asked him if he were the oldest son in his family. Yes, and how had I guessed.

Aimless ambitions give us away every time.

I worked this afternoon with anesthetists in the labor room, and saw a baby born. A full circle from the cardiac arrest. Metempsychosis.

Surgery

October 20

When I told my hostess at dinner last night that I was starting surgery today, she asked, "But where do they get people for you to practice on?"

I replied that I did nothing more ambitious than holding retractors.

Our stand-in preceptor is my friend from pediatrics surgery. "It's perhaps more important in this business to know when *not* to operate." He then took us through the medical conditions that mimic acute appendicitis. Otherwise a "nothing day."

On duty tonight in the emergency room. Saw one patient by myself—an inarticulate Puerto Rican boy with a mysterious ailment of his left ankle. That is the hardest job in medicine: to try to reduce a patient's account of his trouble into something that is brief and accurate, and looks respectable on a chart. After conferring with my elders, I decided that if there was anything wrong with his ankle it was neither acute nor serious, but because he had been using this ailment as an excuse to cut school, I had him sent to orthopedic clinic. Usually my sympathies are on the side of truancy, but I wanted to punish this boy for taking up so much time.

"Should he stop playing football?" his mother asked.

"That's up to him."

I was rescued from this shadow-boxing by a call from the senior resident, who told me he had a patient he wanted me to see. This was a 15-year-old boy with a pain in his right abdomen since last night. I remembered the afternoon lecture and decided that it was probably appendicitis, and that even if it wasn't he would be better off without his appendix. The boy was apprehensive about the operation, and I told him it was not worth worrying about and showed him my own scar. I am not sure if this helped.

The senior resident let me scrub for the operation and serve as "second assistant." ("Keep your hands on the table where I can keep an eye on them.") The incision was only two inches long. ("This is keyhole surgery.") I was practicing the fine art of holding retractors.

In the middle of the operation the patient's pulse began to "bound" to sledgehammer intensity. The abdominal aorta was jiggling the surgeon's hand. I asked the anesthetist if he had ever seen anything like it. No. I pointed out that the patient had been scared. No, that wouldn't account for it. This was a Stepin Fetchit parody of fear. It finally disappeared when they switched anesthetic agents.

The appendix, when we plucked it from the keyhole, looked gratifyingly angry.

We sewed him up and I waited for him to awake so I could tell his mother that all was OK. Funny encounter with the family in the visitors' lounge. The mother wanted to know when he could return to school. The sister, who looked as if she taught school, asked me about the etiology of appendicitis, and finished with, "What is the function of the spleen?" * The father showed the proper perspective toward the evening's events. He was asleep in a chair.

October 21

The patient postappendectomy day No. 1 was not yet himself. I gave him a brief physical exam. His mother had mentioned that a heart murmur had been noted a year ago, and I tried to track this down. For a while I could only find vague swishes, but when I put my stethoscope low on his chest I heard "Flub-dip-dip" instead of the usual "Flub-dip." I called the subintern over to hear it. He, too, missed it on his first attempt and I had to locate it for him. Third-year students are always coming up with murmurs that either don't exist or else don't mean anything, but this was an unmistakable extra "dip." We ordered an EKG.

I made the mistake of asking the boy if there was anything I could do for him. I had to buy him a newspaper and phone his girlfriend Diana.

In surgical pathology class that afternoon we played this game: we would be shown a fresh specimen, and we would have to guess the story of the patient from whom it had been excised, giving his probable sex, age (race and occupation when pertinent), and then describe the course of this illness. The game worked well. The first specimen was a prostate and the second a pair of earlobes. The third was a very familiar-looking appendix.

"This is the appendix of a 15-year-old boy, and his girlfriend's name is Diana."

The class liked it, but our instructor didn't think that was funny at all.

* We dunno.

Surgery

October 22

I was introduced to the world of proctoscopy this afternoon. The proctoscope is an unglamorous instrument but an important one. Cancer of the colon is the single biggest neoplasm of both sexes, and two thirds of the time it occurs within reach of this tool. I tend to shy away from commandments, but I do believe that proctoscopy should be a part of the annual physical exam. There are so many cancers that are hard to spot that it is stupid to miss the easy ones.

Anyway, thanks to this great tool, I was able to help a patient by extracting a fishbone from a most sensitive area. We had first thought it was a pin, and had pricked our fingers on it.

"I just don't know how a pin would have got there," the patient kept protesting.

Yes, he had eaten fish for dinner about five days ago. This was the first cure of my career.

October 23

We played another "game" today on rounds with the chief of the surgery department. He would show us an abdomen, and we would tell him the story of that belly.

He showed me a patient with a broad midline scar, and asked me to recount its history.

I was silent.

"Maybe this will help you: have the patient lift his legs slightly off the bed."

The patient complied, and his scar bulged out like a salami.

The story I should have deduced was that this patient had undergone surgery some time ago for a gastric ulcer, that he had contracted pneumonia postop, that his sutures had given way, and that the tissue there had failed to grow together and had retracted, leaving only skin to cover his intestines in that fault.

The chief, having wrung the right guesses from our group, told us the operations they were considering for tomorrow.

When we left the patient I wished him good luck. It was pointed out to me afterward that this was an ill-chosen valediction.

The games that surgeons play when they want to try to teach something prompted the following reverie.

SURGEON (to class): "I have a playing card in my hand; tell me which card it is."
1ST STUDENT: "The two of clubs."
2ND STUDENT: "The jack of diamonds."
SURGEON: "No, no, no! You're going after this in a hit-or-miss fashion. Approach it logically. The first question you should ask is, 'Is it a red card or a black card?'"
3RD STUDENT: "Is it a red card or a black card?"
SURGEON: "A red card."
1ST STUDENT: "Is it a diamond?"
SURGEON: "No. So it must be a heart. Now, which heart is it most likely to be? . . ."

October 24

My patient with the appendectomy was scheduled to be released during the weekend, when I did not plan to be around. I tried to get the results of his EKG to see if his extra sound was associated with any pathological changes on this recording. The cardiology office was closed when I finally got there, but a friendly subintern helped me interpret the wiggles on the sheet. No pathological changes.

I went in to tell the patient, and I am not sure that was

a good move. He was in the visitors' room, watching TV with the beautiful Diana. I asked Diana to excuse us, and we stepped outside.

It was a mistake to tell him that his murmur was normal because he didn't know he had a murmur. He didn't even know what a murmur was, and now I'm afraid he'll worry about it. I should learn to keep my mouth shut when the patient is happy "in the dark."

October 27

My long and unrewarding study of the French language paid off today in vascular clinic. My patient was a 71-year-old man who had been born in Poland and had lived in France. His English was good, but he reverted to French for *les mots justes*. He had experienced an acute *"sensation de pression"* in his left leg (we had been following him for three years because he no longer had pulses in his lower extremities). After conferring with the resident I decided there was no deterioration of his chronic condition and no signs of the recent episode.

"Do you think it will let me live another year?" he asked, pleading for a stay of execution.

Aim high, I told him. Fifty years.

Tonight, the emergency room, which has an attending surgeon on duty in the evening. Although they are well paid for their time, most men would prefer to be home with their families. One surgeon seems to be on duty every time I am there. He claims he has to work because his wife "likes to buy pretty things," but I suspect he is there because he enjoys it. He certainly enjoys teaching, and he is very good at it.

"A kid lacerated his arm on a chain-link fence. He's going to need a few stitches. Do you want to sew him up?"

I told him I had never sutured before, but I was willing to try.

"We have an axiom in surgery. 'See one, do one, teach one.' This one is yours."

The kid was a tough 13-year-old who looked cooperative, and the wound was on the inside of the arm. If I botched it, it wouldn't make any difference to his career in the movies. I decided that this was as good an opportunity as I would get.

The attending directed me as I injected local anesthesia and he demonstrated the first suture himself. Then he handed me the needle.

I had a little trouble pushing the needle through, and also making the knot. The kid sensed that I was a rookie.

"Why don't you let the older guy finish the job?"

Shut up, kid.

I worked slowly, but soon I had the wound well closed with five stitches. The kid said they were his first stitches. I told him they were my first ones, too. This came as no big news.

October 28

A handsome Syrian attending took our group for an hour and went through the differential diagnosis of GI bleeding.

"Never say GI 'bleed'—that's what you hear commonly but it's wrong. There is no such word in English."

"You mean, sir, that 'bleed' is a verb and not a noun."

"Yes, thank you. It is terrible what they are doing to your English language."

He is a good man. His occasional difficulties with our tongue make him seem less sensitive than he is.

In surgery, this is not a major handicap.

October 29

They discussed the week's batting average in grand rounds today. Not perfect, but quite respectable. In one case that came under the heading "complications" the anesthesiology department had some unflattering things said about it. The anesthetist had a "traumatic" intubation and lacked the sense to get help from his attending. He made it on his fourth try, but what the patient's vocal cords were like at present was a mystery. We weren't sure if he could still talk, you see, because the anesthetist had given him three times the usual dose of curare, which they were unable to reverse pharmacologically. The patient was still on a respirator after 24 hours. The anesthetist had whistled jauntily through the whole procedure and had written in the chart, "Normal intubation, normal extubation."

It was decided to make a report to the department of anesthesiology and to wait for heads to roll.

The message I got was (1) don't be afraid to ask for help when things go wrong, but above all do not persist in error; and (2) don't gloss over your mistakes when writing a note in the chart.

It was exciting to be in on this surgical council of war. Questions like "What's our record on this complication from this procedure?" made me respect the vast number of operations that had been handled by the department as represented in this room. The anesthetists were not the only ones to draw criticism: one of the surgeons had two patients who had "complications" from overhydration.

He blushed when the second one was discussed, and I think this week that his patients will tend to be just a little bit thirsty.

October 30

Got to see the greatest feat of God—vascular surgery. A fourth-year student talked me into taking his place as second assistant. My only alternative was a morning of playing guessing games with the head of the department. This was more fun.

The patient was an old man who had suffered a stroke. X-rays showed an obstruction in the left subclavian artery (at the level of the collarbone, carrying blood to the arm); through the collateral circulation this had resulted in a diversion of blood from the right side of the brain.

An incision in the neck was made and the surgical guessing game began:

"What structure is my assistant looking out for now?"

"What would happen to the patient if we cut this?"

We planned to put a shunt between the left carotid and the left subclavian, thus bypassing the obstruction. After inspecting the vessels and deciding it was worth a try, we covered up the neck incision and moved to the thigh. We removed part of the great saphenous vein (a superficial vessel that is used in arterial replacements). One key thing: we marked the direction of the flow with a thread at one end. Veins have one-way valves, and if you put them in the wrong way this is a disaster. The vein looked tiny, but it swelled to sausage size when inflated.

When we returned to the vessels of the neck, I was pessimistic. The graft looked flimsy, and the arteries did not look as if they would welcome the addition. If so much as a needle were passed through them we all got blood on our glasses. I felt sure I was going to witness my first death on the table.

They had me holding retractors with both hands. One was holding the jugular vein out of the way; the other clamped the carotid artery. This was a tricky business in ideal conditions, but my troubles were compounded. I felt faint, because I had not had a drop of water since the preceding evening and because I am not used to vascular surgery. I also had a slight cold: my nose was running and a sneeze was looming on the horizon.

The surgeons made their incision and started suturing the graft into place with a tiny needle and very fine thread. Again, it looked impossible for the one ever to be fitted to the other in a leakproof fashion. I gritted my teeth and promised myself a first-class lunch if I got through without dishonor.

My two afflictions must have canceled each other out: I neither fainted nor sneezed. The suturing worked. The joints were not leakproof at first; when they were first tested by releasing the clamp, rivulets of blood would stream through them, but additional sutures stemmed the flow. When the surgeons were finished they let me admire the new piece of plumbing. I told them I was impressed. Then they sewed up the incisions, one working at the neck, the other at the thigh, while I cut the sutures for them one centimeter above the knot. You have to start somewhere.

I enjoyed changing out of my "white pajamas" at noon, looking down on the bright and busy city below, with the satisfaction of a good morning's work behind me.

October 31

Our preceptor took us to see the city hospital where he has a post. This hospital used to evoke memories of certain health facilities as photographed by Mathew Brady. It has since moved to a new building—an architectural leapfrog of one hundred years. The new hospital is a rarity in that it seems a pleasant place to work and even to be sick in. For the interior color scheme, the traditional anemic green has been broken down, and a strong yellow and blue complement the fresh white walls and ceiling. The only mistake the architects made is that the patients are the same as in the old building. The average patient may be the same as anywhere else, but there are enough "really sick" people here to put this hospital in a special class. The characteristic feature of this patient population is that, for one reason or another, they are late in getting medical care. Problems come in already out of control.

And so rounds today featured several candidates for the Pathology Hall of Fame. The chief of service is a handsome patrician who looks slightly out of place in these surroundings. At one point he had to criticize an intern for his technique in changing dressings:

"Those rubber gloves, which started out sterile, lost some of that magical quality on the way to the wound."

The intern was not as embarrassed as he should have been.

I had a free lunch in the cafeteria with some medical interns (who tend to be brighter than their surgical colleagues). They have a good esprit and a range of conversation, and I am tempted to join them in two years' time.

The drawback, though, is that it is easy here to become casual about sterile gloves.

November 3

Our preceptor asks us about our patients. Two points emerge:

(1) Always ask the patient directly about the onset of his present disease, and do not rely on what is recorded in the admission note in the chart. Stories expand when pressure is released.

(2) In "following" a surgical patient the physical examination is more important than the laboratory data.

Simple points, but "well worth keeping in mind." Our

preceptor can repeat them without being pedantic. He is a highly civilized man.

November 4, Election Day

I got turkeyed into working in the blood-chemistry lab all today, because the usual staff was given a holiday. There was a lot of work to do, but I did not mind the quantity as much as the fact that specimens were sent down throughout the day instead of all at once. Chemistry is like cooking, and it is a lot easier to bake six angel cakes together than three at different times. I was furious, because I knew that these "emergencies" were not emergencies at all, but tests that could have been done routinely if the doctors had come in on time.

On the other hand, I know that I will be abusing technicians in two years.

In either case I would be much happier if hospitals closed down on holidays. Patients are tyrants.

November 5

A grateful patient showed me how to make a phone call for only one nickel. The patient is a college student who has recovered from whatever was wrong with him and is due to go home soon. I have done nothing to him or for him, and that is why he is grateful.

The trick is to punch the coin release just after dropping the nickel. My friend has come close to perfecting his technique in the course of his two-month hospital stay. I grasp the principle, but cannot make it work. I will save it for true nickel emergencies or a protracted illness of my own.

We have a pedagogic discussion of the history of cardiac surgery. Heroics; not for me though. The X-ray of an implanted pacemaker looks as if someone is trying to smuggle a transistor radio in his chest. We are told that the pacer can become dislodged and can set the diaphragm contracting at 72 beats per minute. We find this hilariously funny.

November 6

The chief of service gave us a chance to learn from someone else's mistake today. The only problem was that we could not identify the error. A patient in the recovery room, postsurgery, had developed severe complications of such nature as to point an accusing finger at the anesthesiologist. We all tried to figure out what went wrong, but each hypothesis required a freak occurrence or else the anesthetist's negligence. The patient looked done for, but I hope my impressions are wrong.

This is an admirable part of the profession: the advertisement of mistakes in an effort to figure out why they happened and to alert others to the danger. This is kept within the profession; whether the family or the general public should receive the same reports is a more controversial issue.

We had a seminar on the problem of telling a patient he has cancer: our idealism versus the experience of a chest surgeon, a psychiatrist, and the hospital chaplain. The students turned out to be more "sensitive" and less inclined to tell the patient "the truth." The three pros felt that (1) The diagnosis of cancer is not a death sentence. Patients can go on for years, with or without pain, whatever the statistical "prognosis." (2) Patients sense the diagnosis anyway, in spite of the charades of doctor and family. (3) Not to tell a patient implies that you are afraid of the disease. Telling him implies that you are in control and is actually more reassuring.

The chaplain pointed out that people used to die at

Surgery

home, and now they come to hospitals to die. The ministry of medicine.

November 7

The chief resident took us down to see the X-rays of a patient who had come in last night. The patient had a perforated duodenal ulcer, and a good way to verify that is to spot air under the diaphragm on an upright chest film. We will be given a quickie course in radiology in the spring, but I am glad to pick up what I can along the way.

The room where the X-rays were read had a quotation from *Macbeth* taped to the shelf:

"Hence, horrible shadow . . . Unreal mockery, hence!"

The main attraction of thyroid clinic later was a gypsy woman. She had a tumor removed years ago, and kept her follow-up appointments faithfully. This time she was brought in by her son, who had a leather jacket and a ducktail haircut and looked tough enough to dissuade me from palpating his mother's neck.

"The first thing to remember about gypsies," our attending said when they had left, "is to have nothing to do with them. When one comes into the hospital the whole tribe comes with him. When they decide that the treatment has run its course, they leave, taking the patient with them. And always check your wallet!"

One doctor had a reflex tester which gave an EKG-type reading on the ankle jerk. The greater the thyroid hormone levels, the faster the reflex. When these first came out, we were told, doctors used them to differentiate hypothyroid, euthyroid, and hyperthyroid patients. There is too much overlap between these categories for reliability, but the machine can be used to test a patient against himself. This doctor uses it to "follow" his thyroid patients, instead of drawing a blood test which costs the patient $15 and takes a week to yield its results. Tricks like these make a competent doctor more than just competent.

It was a good clinic. I learned that a thyroid nodule is probably not cancer, and that if it is cancer you can still have a long and happy life. I suppose I had read that before, but now it's a feeling in my bones.

November 8

Last Saturday of the hypnosis course. Miss Johnson of Masters and Johnson fame came to talk about her approach in therapy for sexual problems. Her therapeutic approach had absolutely nothing to do with hypnosis but I was glad to hear her. She is a fine lady, much to my surprise. Sexy too.

The hypnosis course may be the best course of my life. At the end of it, though, we were very tired of the subject. From being skeptical at first we had reached the point where we took it all for granted, where everything the teacher said seemed obvious. That is a sure sign that we have "had the course," and I look forward to the same sensation in some medical specialty some fine day.

November 9

It's Sunday, and I have a hangover, and I have to work in the lab. Blood chemistry, my own and others, occupies the entire day.

I wish I was rich.

November 10

Went down to the city hospital and saw some "trauma" cases. In most places this means victims of speeding automobiles but here they are mainly victims of speeding bullets. These people are pretty miserable for a fortnight, but if they make it to the hospital conscious they seem to survive.

I decided it was a question of an initiation rite on both sides: they do not consider themselves men until they have been shot, and we do not consider ourselves men until we have handled a shooting emergency.

"What are you going to do if a guy comes in with blood pouring out of his belly and you are alone in the emergency room?" This is asked by skeptical friends and self-questioning nightmares. I will be ready because an intern at this hospital told us what to do, and it is inscribed in my black book:

- A—Airway, insure adequate
- B—Breathing, insure adequate
- C—Circulation, insure adequate
- T—Type & crossmatch (draw blood for this and other tests)
- I—IV's, start them (usually with Ringer's lactate solution)
- N—Nasogastric tube, to empty stomach preanesthesia
- C—Catheterize bladder and send off specimen for urinalysis
- T—Tell nurse to "prep" patient for operation

I am now ready for the initiation rite.
A-B-C-T-I-N-C-T

November 11

Grand Rounds. Another "severe complication," this time resulting in death. Also mysterious, but there is one element in common with the last case: the anesthesiologist is the same. I am glad I am not in his shoes.

Our preceptor shows us a 45-year-old woman with a lump in her breast. On palpation there is a baseball-sized mass. She will be operated on today.

"I just hope I can keep the breast." She is very nervous.

Outside, our preceptor explains that the lump seems to be cancerous and the lesion too far advanced for surgery. However, they will take a biopsy today just to be sure. He recommends that one of us follow the patient.

Later I follow the patient up to the OR and watch the biopsy. They take a nick near the surface and hand it to the pathologist. In five minutes the specimen is freeze-dried and microscopic slides are prepared. I look at this under medium power. As we suspected, the lady can keep her breast.

November 12

I got talked into holding retractors for a radical mastectomy. The fourth-year student had been the second assistant for enough of these so that he never wanted to see another. In other words, he had done one before. I too could have lived happily without this experience, but I decided that it would do me less harm than him, and scrubbed up.

I am glad I did. My only previous contact with mastectomies was watching from a gallery for five minutes, and it was not a pretty sight. Before, I was afraid of the operation. Now, after four upright hours of holding hooks, I know that this operation is nothing to be afraid of. It is just a big pain in the neck.

The worst part about the whole procedure is that there is no simple way to avoid it, such as giving up smoking or the like. Not even early detection will help. The only way to get around the operation is to hide the tumor until it has advanced so far that surgery will not help. (I guess I will never be a surgeon since the prevention of disease interests me more than specious surgical treatment.)

Pedagogy in the operating theater. The scrub nurse teaches a nursing student how to give us our sterile gloves and gowns. It is like the training of a geisha—silent and cheerfully subservient.

The attending teaches the resident how to slice. (Later the resident complains, "He tells me to cut thicker. The last guy told me to make it thinner. I wish I could train with just one guy.")

The resident teaches me how to hold skin hooks. "Direct the tension up, like this. Good boy."

I am 25 years old, and I wonder if I am to spend my life in an eternal apprenticeship.

November 13

Got a look at some patients who did not have breast surgery in time. I now have a higher opinion of the radical mastectomy. A most depressing disease in any form and with any therapy. We are told to be optimistic when talking to patients. This may take some acting but it sounds worthwhile.

We were told of new nonsurgical approaches to treatment. These are now used in metastatic disease, but could in the next millennium replace the radical operation. One interested me particularly. Interferon is a protein made by cells to stop viral infections. It is thought that breast cancer may be a viral infection, and it has been demonstrated that interferon can stop breast cancer in mice. The big problems with this substance are: (1) Production. Interferon to be used in humans must be made by human cells, which really turn out one crop in their lifetime. (2) Storage. Interferon is unstable, loses its activity even when stored in the freezer. (3) Inactivation. Interferon has a half-life of a few minutes in the body.

We were told that a researcher on our staff had solved one of these problems and was planning to run the first human tests in a couple of years. This happened to be a man I know, and whose intricately equipped lab I was always meaning to have explained to me, only I had never got around to it. I will now pay closer attention to his research, and may even do an elective with him next year. This seems as if it may point toward a way of keeping people out of operating rooms.

I went around to see my friend in his lab and listened to him talk of his research. He is old, but he is satisfied. And confident.

November 14

The senior resident displayed his true turkey nature today. We were discussing the indications for limb amputation which include cancer, wet gangrene, and "intractable pain."

I asked if in the latter case they would try hypnosis before they unsheathed their knives.

"I don't think any serious psychiatrist would attempt hypnosis in such a case."

I pointed out that where pain was the only problem there would be nothing to lose from an attempt at hypnotherapy.

The resident doubted if they could get anyone to take the time required to hypnotize such a patient.

I replied that it could be done in fifteen minutes, and that you could determine instantly (via the eye signs) whether the patient was hypnotizable.

The resident said it sounded like a lot of mumbo jumbo.

It is a lot of mumbo jumbo, but the point is that this mumbo jumbo may work and save a gruesome operation. I did not expect the resident to be converted to hypnosis, but I was annoyed at his closed-minded rejection of this approach, about which he knew little indeed. Surgeons tend to be smug; they have no humility before the unknown.

The resident did finally concede that, yes, maybe hypnosis should be considered before surgery. Pyrrhic victory.

At the end of the day I was on duty at the chemistry lab in the other hospital. I was delivering the "slips" (the results of the tests) to the wards when I was stopped by a patient who saw my white coat and begged for help. This man had a cancer which involved his larynx and esophagus, and had had operations to bypass these structures—the former via a tracheostomy, the latter via a hose of skin which went from his mouth to his sternum. He was a pitiful sight, and previously when I had come across him it was a struggle not to stare too hard. This time he had tears in his eyes and was pointing to his bandaged head. Little puffs of sound spurted from his tracheostomy; they only added to his distress. He clasped his hands, genuflected, and begged with his eyes for assistance. The appeal came through, but I had no idea what he wanted. More puffs of sound. I seized a paper napkin and a pen and got the following:

Please Help me to light tight

so I wrote underneath

IS YOUR BANDAGE TOO TIGHT?
Yes ☐
No ☐

He answered yes.

The nurse, sitting unmoved at the station, told me not to worry about him. (She had been following him for a year.) I would have to be made of stronger stuff than titanium to ignore him, so I told her to call the doctor.

She said he was on his way, and he was. I turned the problem over to him and returned to the lab.

Discussion: Is life so dear . . . ?

November 17

Went down to the other city hospital and saw, among others, an old man with both legs in casts. For his history, he seemed fairly cheerful. He had come into the hospital for some problem stemming from his alcoholism and poverty. The effect of this combination on his mind, however, had been underrated. In the course of his treatment he found his way onto a hospital roof and took a swan dive of some six stories. He was brought to the emergency room shouting, "I'm coming to you, Jesus." The ER staff, however, had lost one "urban paratrooper" just an hour before and were determined not to let Jesus get this one too. This man had both feet hanging by skin flaps, fractures of the pelvis, hips, and ribs. Because of the previous case everybody happened to be right there, including a neurologist, a vascular surgeon, and an anesthesiologist, and they went to work. The humanoids won.

After the presentation, I asked the intern:

"This may seem like a naive question, but did we do this guy a favor?"

The intern said that was a good point.

November 18

Surgical pathology is just like the first two years—you sit and get talked at for three hours (actually two and a half, but it seems like four). I decided that I am in the wrong field, because pathology bores the hell out of me. For each disease we get: sex ratio, peak age incidence, contributing factors, theories of etiology, microscopic and gross appearance, clinical symptoms, X-rays, and treatment, medical and surgical.

I look forward to the year 3000 and the eradication of disease. A course of surgical pathology will be restricted to a discussion of the pathogenesis of freckles. The new Jerusalem.

November 19

The first principle of modern medicine is that the patient must wait. I spent the day with the resident who makes the decisions about clinic patients whose ailments may require hospitalization for general surgery. At noon, having seen three patients for about ten minutes each, he said, "I'm going to lunch." There were six other charts on his desk, and each chart represented a patient who was going to miss lunch in the hope that he might soon be called.

Two hours later the resident returned from his repast. The charts on his desk were now an even dozen. Hearing his name on page he asked the operator for the extension and dialed it. He reached the lady who runs the part of the clinic whose phone was ten feet away.

"Why did you put me on page?"

"All these patients are waiting and I was worried that you weren't coming back from lunch."

"In the future don't worry." His tone was one of an officer reprimanding a subordinate for allowing humanitarian feelings to interfere with warfare.

The resident began to work his way through the pile. The first patient was an 80-year-old woman with signs of intestinal obstruction. She and her husband had been waiting since 8 o'clock.

"I'm sorry you had to wait so long. I got held up in another part of the hospital." (The cafeteria?)

"Oh, no, doctor, don't worry on our account."

The couple were actually apologetic.

I was disgusted. I will admit that careful treatment is more important than fast treatment. Having people wait also discourages them from coming in with trivial complaints. But the current contempt for the patient's time may discourage sick people from getting any treatment at all.

November 20

A young Spanish couple are brought to the emergency room with broken ankles and small lacerations. They were having an argument and the woman had jumped out of the window. The man had followed her. Fortunately, they had been on the second floor. Lucky in love.

November 21

Open-heart surgery again. I wisely decided not to scrub. The third-year student is tolerated in ordinary operations, and occasionally even useful. Here he would only get in the way: there were four doctors scrubbed in and there just was not room. Besides, the surgeons had something to worry about that required their total attention.

The patient was a middle-aged man who had worked his heart out in a steel mill. (Heart surgeons get rich off steelworkers.) I was glad to find that the tape deck had been retired in favor of a radio. It was still the same kind of un-music; the big difference was that you did not hear the same cycle repeated eight times, and you could not predict what song was coming next. The Great Conductor manifested his work at the critical point in the operation: from the radio came the theme from the James Bond movie *You Only Live Twice*.

The translation of the original haiku:

Surgery

> *You only live twice*
> *Once when you are born*
> *Once when you look death in the face.*

And at that point they started the pump.

November 24

Vascular clinic today. I see the patients alone first, then again with the attending. My first patient was an old lady who had arterial problems in her legs. A year ago she could not walk half a block without stopping to rest her legs; now, with medication, she was able to walk ten. She had stopped smoking a month ago because of a "lung infection." She says she feels much better, but still has to fight the urge for a cigarette. I urged her to keep her record clean. I spent a good while talking to her and felt it was justified. Cigarettes are a threat to anyone according to statistics; to these people they are directly harmful. (Nicotine causes a spasm of the arterial wall, further limiting circulation.) Preventive surgery. I thought that cigarettes might have something to do with her "lung infection," since lung cancer often presents as pneumonia. I suggested that she be given a repeat X-ray (her last one was two years ago) but the resident shrugged off the idea. That is one of the problems with medical centers; the patient is treated in his several parts, never in the whole.

The next patient was a young androgyne who was worried about his varicose veins. It was hard to tell which factor was more important: the pain or the cosmetic aspect. He wanted a vein-stripping operation to be followed by plastic surgery.

"I realize that it will be expensive and take a long time," he said, batting his eyelashes.

He must also have realized that it will be painful. We approved the vein-stripping operation, but told him that for plastic surgery he was on his own. That is, he would have to find a surgeon who believed in money as one of the indications for operating.

November 25

I received my first issue of the *New England Journal of Medicine,* which comes out weekly. The *NEJM* is authoritative and well edited, and the student subscription is only $5 a year. I should have started my subscription two years ago. It is not enough to know what the textbooks say on any one topic; I should know what the latest journal article says as well (and there is a lot of "Journalsmanship" in medicine, articles cited on rounds or in the chart). Without this "current" communication, the medical profession would revert to the situation found at the turn of the century: a few (lucky) maestros and a lot of hacks.

The parts of each issue that I actually like to *read* are the letters (where nit-picking is king, and the sarcasm is British in its understatement) and the clinicopathological conference. The CPC reads like the synopsis of a murder mystery. First the "murder": the patient's history, physical, lab findings, and hospital course are presented in a summary which usually ends with the sentence "Resuscitation procedures were unsuccessful, and the patient expired on the seventy-eighth hospital day." This gives us the corpse and most of the data. A doctor from the faculty of Harvard Medical School then theorizes for several pages about which disease (or form of therapy) was the source of the patient's afflictions, and he is forced to make a diagnosis at the end. The consensus of the medical students is then announced by their representative, with only a tad more pomposity than the occasion demands. A few other doctors are allowed to stick their neck out, and then, with all bets on the table, the pathologist makes his report. This is accepted as the ultimate, true, real diagnosis. The armchair detectives are right better than half the time. This is an instructive game to play; very rarely in medicine can you learn what is "really" going on. Or went on.

Many medical schools, hospitals, and medical societies have such clinicopathological clinics, and they keep the profession self-critical and alert. We have them at our medical center, every week for an hour, and I enjoy them mainly because it is the only time that the medical-school community comes together. I think I learn more, though, from the ones in the *New England Journal of Medicine*. When I read them.

November 26

My last day in surgery. We had an oral exam which was not too ferocious: four students versus three surgeons. They showed me an X-ray revealing gallstones, and asked me what I would predict regarding the history and present illness of the patient, and how I would treat this. The hardest part of the exam was trying not to answer the easy questions aimed at other students. I did OK, and I learned something. A good exam.

I dropped by to visit the steelworker whose heart operation I had watched a few days ago. He was looking fine. I asked him if he was going to return to work (that's how well he looked).

"No, I'm retired, and I plan to spend my time fishing, in the hills in back of my home. No more steel mill. Just me and the mountains."

I felt surgery had done well by us both.

Ear, Nose, and Throat
and a Little Ophthalmology

December 1

Do unto others on ENT. The first day we practiced on each other. My throat was good to look down because I have only a slight gag reflex. When I tried my partner, the combination of my clumsiness and her hyperreflexion was too much. Our attending volunteered to "sit" for me.

I got the little mirror back there and looked.

"See the cords?" asked the resident, who was watching me.

"Only the tongue depressor."

I monkeyed around some more without results.

Finally the attending came up spluttering, "I'm good but I'm not that good."

On my third try (he was a very dedicated ENT man) I was able to see the cords, a fish mouth of yellow ivory, opening and closing with his voice. It was worth all the annoyance I caused him.

Inspected the operating-room microscope. A $5 bill under this gadget is fun to play with. I read the names of the states inscribed on the Lincoln Memorial, and glimpsed the outline of the great statue within. The engraving actually looks coarse at moderate magnification. We were invited to prove our dexterity by carving a moustache on the head of a coin, but I passed this up.

The afternoons of this relaxed week are spent on ophthalmology. One lecture on how to examine the eye and another on optometry. Plug for contact lenses. I wondered about my chances of talking this doctor into giving me a free set. Probably slim.

December 2

Had our lecture on the ear today. We must have had six lectures in the first year on the physiology of hearing; for the clinical problems of this organ we get only one. Science marches on.

I was impressed with the fact that the lecturer talked of fractions of tenths of millimeters. These surgeons are the jewelers of medicine.

In the clinic I got a patient who had come in two weeks ago complaining of nausea, headache, and occasional vomiting, and had been kicked around from service to service. I made the mistake of trying to figure out what was wrong with her, instead of just looking at her from an ENT point of view. She did have gallstones and may have been pregnant, but the attending was not as interested in these explanations as he was by the fact that she had a lump in the nasopharynx. He told me afterward that it was probably cancer, but that it might respond to radiation, so her face would be intact.

The importance of tunnel vision.

December 4

"Are you a physician?" a well-dressed elderly man asks me as I am leaving ENT clinic.

"Well, yes."

"Is this the region of the ethmoid sinus?" he inquires, pointing to the bridge of his nose.

"Yes." This was a calculated risk on my part. I knew that there was a sinus in that region, and that one of the nasal sinuses was termed the ethmoid.

"One of your physicians here pushed the bone in on this side. He was examining me at the time."

There was a slight depression there, resembling the effect of wearing glasses. Yes, he did wear glasses. Six months ago he had slipped on the steps in front of the hospital, resulting in the fracture of his jaw and some loose teeth. The hospital persuaded him to accept free treatment for his ensuing problems instead of suing for damages. This man took them up on their offer, although he lives 200 miles away. He came here today to get some teeth pulled, and just stopped by this clinic to see what we had to say.

I could have taken him into the clinic without an appointment and asked an attending to examine him. But he put up his hand to his nose at the mention of the word "examination," as if he wanted to protect it from us. I asked him to list the ways in which this bothered him; the aggregate of complaints was not very impressive. I decided that this was a "dog," told him not to worry about it, and if it bothered him in the future he should be sure to come back. That was just what he wanted to hear. He thanked me warmly.

I told him I had gone to college in his region; he guessed the college and added that he had taken a summer school course there in organic chemistry. I had taken the same summer school course, so we had a reunion. ("Best course of my life, demanding, but if you get through it you can do anything.")

I asked if he had gone on in chemistry.

No, his career had been in cost accounting. He was retired now; his hobby was the structure of atoms and molecules. He had even written a paper on the hydrogen atom.

I asked if I could give him my address so he could send me a copy.

"As a matter of fact, I have a copy right here." He pulled out some Xeroxed sheets from his breast pocket.

It began: "My theory about the structure of and motions in the hydrogen atom H^1 is as follows . . ."

December 5

Last day of this week. Got the pitch from both the ENT and ophthalmology departments.

"I remember when I was finished with ENT," one of the attendings mused, with an accent you could chin yourself upon. "I was a fourth-year student in Germany, and I asked myself, 'How can anybody be so stupid to spend his life in this field?' Then the war broke out. The doctors went to the front and we took their place in the hospitals. I was put in charge of a 50-bed ENT ward. I had finished the course the week before. I'll never forget my first tonsillectomy. Blood everywhere. The patient did fine, but I don't see how I ever survived."

This man is one of the few free spirits in medicine. He gets the same charge from restoring eardrums as the toymakers in the storybooks do from fixing dolls. ENT has the advantage of offering a lot to the patient for very little work. It is also a very independent field: many of the operations can be done without an assistant.

The ophthalmologists were a little more selective.

"Frankly, you have to be a compulsive neurotic for this field."

I tried to picture myself in this light, but even with the amplification of fantasy my level of compulsive neurosis was barely enough to make me a good garbage man.

"We find the people who made models when boys do

well in this field. You have to be good with your hands. Also, you have to have good vision. I know of one top man who is color-blind (he told me in secret). That is a big disadvantage. But depth perception is especially important. We once had to let a resident go because he was deficient in this one area. He was a good man, but he had ruined too many eyes."

We were allowed to play with their $5000 operating microscope. This makes the ENT one look like a hand lens. I focused on the glass eye that was in the field, and picked up the tiny threaded needle with the thin forceps. I'm afraid I lack the touch, because the grasp of the forceps tiddlywinked the needle out of sight.

Neurology

December 8

It is nice to get back to a clinical ward.

"The first rule on this floor," the resident tells us, "is to stay out of the nurses' way."

A youngish grand old man shows us how to do a neurological history and physical. He is a great clinician, but he looks like a shoemaker in a Walt Disney movie, thanks to his half-framed glasses, hunched frame, and rolled-up shirt sleeves. He is beloved of children and small dogs, and smiles sincerely if somewhat mechanically after each sentence.

"Anything takes time, so you might as well do it the right way. At least you're rewarded. If you do it this way, it may be hard at first, but it will get easy as pie after a while."

I look at this expert/simpleton and I believe it.

"I don't believe in textbooks. Most of the people who write textbooks don't examine patients. They're too busy reading other books and copying."

He tells us to record our history of the present illness with a paragraph for each symptom-complaint.

"If you write a history that way, you can get all the facts down without having to compete with, say, Hemingway." (Who must have been the subject of a few write-ups himself.)

He then shows us how to do a complete neuro exam in ten minutes. Very speedy.

"If any of you knew this now, I'd be afraid of you. I'd shun you. I'd say there's something wrong with that guy. You pick all this up as you go along."

That would be nice.

December 9

Today we got to watch the shoemaker at work. The residents had selected a patient and they gave him a brief history. This patient had been hit by a car six months ago.

The shoemaker's hands flew to his temple.

"This guy is going to be tricky. I just know I'm going to have a migraine all day."

He went on to explain the cause of his worries.

"You've got to be on the lookout for *malingering* and conversion hysteria in the following situations: (a) in the military, (b) in situations involving compensation and disability, (c) in auto accidents and anywhere there will be extensive litigation.

"I *never* accept a case where litigation is involved. I've even turned down doctors' families."

When the patient was led in, I would have awarded him $100,000 on the basis of his limp alone. There were other things wrong with him as well. But the shoemaker was not so impressed with these ailments. Whenever he came across a weakness or pain, he would have the patient repeat the original maneuver indirectly in going through a different action. Lo and behold, when the patient was

Neurology

thus distracted the finding would disappear. The examiner thanked him for his cooperation, watched him get dressed again, and closed the door as he limped out.

"Malingering! Did you see the way he wriggled on his slippers when he couldn't move his foot before!" After cataloguing the inconsistencies uncovered, he told us his thoughts on the subject.

"Malingering is just as much a disease as conversion hysteria. I never diagnosed a case of malingering in the army. It is a court-martial offense. Whenever I saw it, I called it 'conversion hysteria.' I didn't feel like tying up the rest of my life in testimony.

"If you are dealing with a patient who is malingering, never let on that you know. He's got to have a way to save face. And never, never tell the family.

"These people can be very easy to cure. Almost anything will work (if applied with a straight face). One of our residents has Charcot's original apparatus. The patient holds the two wires to his hands, while the doctor turns the crank of the magneto. A magical current effects the cure, but make sure you don't electrocute the patient.

"My old mentor used to collect this kind of patient. He had a collection of crutches in his office rivaling that of St. Anne de Beaupré."

December 10

The chief resident's office. A cubbyhole lined with the autographed pictures of previous chief residents. Like the list of Heads of School. On the desk a plastic gold sword, named Excalibur, with the explanatory note "For use in times of crisis." If I have a minute I might want to look at the old group picture. Yes. The grand old men as young hotshots. Smiling and sure of themselves.

We talk about books. He has written a "semihistorical" novel about the development of a miracle drug that he worked on. He is now trying to get it published. I tell him about my journal. We are allies in our literary pretensions, but I wish I had some of his skill.

On the ward at night. Like a ghost ship. I don't know if it is because of sedation or old age, but the whole ward is asleep under the lights at 9 o'clock—everyone, that is, except one black man sitting upright on the edge of his chair, glancing at the door. I learn later of his many attempts at escape.

The nurse asks me to look at a patient. Mr. Duvalos, bodega owner, is in "shock" and says he is going to die. I realize I don't have the first idea about how to thwart this prediction. I tell the nurse to call the resident on duty tonight, and I take the vital signs.

"Patient Duvalos complaining of chest pains," I report to the resident. "Afebrile, pulse 112, blood pressure 160/90, respiration 36. Also, he had a dream."

"What was the dream?"

"That he is going to die tonight."

"Oh, no," the resident corrected me. "No, sir. Not tonight. Not when I'm on duty."

With the aid of an EKG, his chest X-ray, a medical consultation, and a wonderful drug called digitalis, we made sure that it would not be tonight.

December 11

The curse of alcohol, manifested in two ways:

(1) A patient who is a chronic alcoholic (he admits to a quart of wine per day). An alcoholic is someone who drinks more than his doctor. Although I have been known to drink a quart of wine, my intervals are somewhat longer. Patient came to us complaining of decrease of vision and burning sensation of the feet. Also said he "walks funny," so that people think he's drunk all the time. Examination revealed atrophy of his optic nerve, a

"stocking-glove" peripheral neuritis of all four extremities, and decreased cerebellar functions. Our attending of the morning happened to be doing research on the cerebellum, and gave us a quick review of the subject. Main point: the grape does more than cause cirrhosis.

(2) I went to a cocktail party given by an old girlfriend. Usually I am slow to reveal the fact that I am a medical student to people my own age because girls tend to get suddenly interested and men tend to get somewhat competitive. Unfortunately, my ex-girlfriend's mother had let the cat out of the bag in a way that made me feel self-conscious. After my second Americano, I remember myself telling tales of the hospital to a wide-eyed young lady. I also recall the blistering look of contempt in the face of the guy she was with. I deserved it. Never again. Doctors should be solitary drinkers.

December 12

The initial part of the neurological examination is the test of mental status. Most physicians will check to see if the patient knows who he is, where he is, and what day of the week it is. If the patient performs creditably during this interrogation, he is said to be "Alert and Oriented X 3," and on to the next part. Real neurologists, however, should be more exacting in their evaluation. In learning to check the mental status these were my first set of responses. The patient was Ulysses Bell. He had some of the noble qualities of Jack Johnson, but I was afraid he would detect my impertinence and tear me apart.

(1) Attention span, easily tested by asking patient to subtract serial 7's from 100.
    Q. "What's 7 from 100?"
    A. "75."
    Q. "What's 7 from 75?"

A. "75."
Q. "What's 10¢ from one dollar?"
A. "85¢."
(2) Mood—ask patient how he feels.
Q. "How do you feel?"
A. "How do you feel?"
(3) Memory.
Q. "What did you have for breakfast?"
A. "85¢."
(4) Manipulation of old knowledge.
Q. "Why do people wear wristwatches?"
A. "I don't know."
(5) Possible aphasia.
Patient is shown a nickel and asked to identify it.
A. "85¢ take away a nickel."
Final inquiry.
Q. "Are you putting me on?"
A. (Looking into examiner's eye) "Are you putting me on?"

December 15

I found out that Mr. Bell had a frontal-lobe tumor and was exhibiting classical "perseveration," or repetition. I asked him to write his name three times for me, adding one, two, and finally four extra l's at the end. Binary progression, you see.

The protocol for grand rounds this morning:

Patient: 40-year-old white man.
Chief complaint: lack of ambition—2 years' duration.
Present illness: 2½ years PTA (previous to admission)—patient became less critical in his thinking—something unusual for a professor of mathematics. He developed difficulty in keeping up with the students in his course.

Physical exam: Normal.
Neuro exam: Jovial inappropriate affect. Poor hop.

The man turned out to have a serious disease.

December 16

Medical students should be given a stipend of $2000 per year.

Our resident is annoyed at us for delaying our write-ups of newly admitted patients. Our schedule is so packed that we are busy all day until 4 o'clock. I have to work at my paying job all this week from 5 to midnight. That leaves me an hour in the afternoon or the first 7 hours of the morning in which to do my complete history, physical, and neuro examinations on any patient I admit. Why do I work at the lab job? To eat and pay the rent.

"Let's get those work-ups done *fast*."

I point out that some of us have jobs at night.

"You have to make up your mind what you're here for—is it to become a doctor or is it to make money."

Hmmm . . .

December 17

An admission I was unable to duck turned out to be an interesting one. (Interesting to us, that is.)

A middle-aged accountant came in with a tremor and progressive absent-mindedness of a year's duration. He didn't come in by himself—his family and GP had led him to us.

I made the mistake of trying to get a complete history from him. I should have asked his wife. One of this guy's characteristics is a slowness of motion and of speech. He would look straight at me when I asked him a question, but his gaze would shift to the distance as he tried to formulate his answer. I would wait until I decided that I really didn't care about that question, and would start to ask him another one.

"No, I'm still working on the first one. Let's see now, when was it?"

At first I thought that his careful memory searches were a part of his professional background. (He is the first male adult I have admitted.) I soon decided that this was part of his pathology. To elicit the history of the present illness had taken me over two hours.

The patient seemed not to care about his illness. Also part of his pathology.

December 18

I found out today just how far his apathy extended. He needed a spinal tap done as a part of his work-up. The resident had said I could do it. It was to be my first.

I went to the patient's bedside.

"Come on, Mr. Marks, we're going to do a spinal tap."

He sat up and blinked a few times. Then asked, "Who does 'we' include?"

I told him myself and the resident, which was the truth.

We got him on the table and had him bend forward. The resident was holding him in position. I was palpating the lumbar spine, figuring where I was going to plant my needle.

Suddenly he turned and faced me.

"Just a minute, Mr. MacNab, do you have an MD?"

"Sure he does," said the resident.

"Actually, I am just locating the interspace," I reassured him. "Dr. Abbot will do the actual tap."

I made sure that I stayed in front of him until the tap was finished. Lumbar punctures are painful experiences, and I did not want to increase his apprehension.

Afterward, the resident criticized me for being buffaloed by the patient. I replied that there were some people I could con, but not him. Not for my first tap, anyway.

December 19

Two quotations.

The chief resident, last week:

"We are living in a Puritan society in which disease is a punishment for sin, and neurological disease is a particularly severe punishment."

A handsome black paraplegic (he had been shot in the back by a policeman):

"I must have done some powerful sinning to get wired up this way." (Quizzical smile.) "I'm still praying, though."

January 5, 1970

Back to work after the last Christmas vacation of my life. There are some advantages to being a student.

Worked up a 74-year-old man who has nothing much wrong with him. A tall and charming Irishman who for 40 years worked as a cable splicer under the city's streets. The fact that there is almost nothing wrong with him makes him the aristocrat of the ward.

He was a treat to examine. He had left school at 11, some 60 years ago, but he was sharp. He breezed through serial 7's from 100 (Alertness) and "the last five presidents" (Memory), and was explaining the meaning of specific proverbs (Abstract Thinking).

Suddenly he realized the impertinence of my "evaluation of mental status," and turned on me with a smile.

"What are you asking me all these questions for? I'd like to see you do the Jumble I did today."

The Jumble is an anagram newspaper feature. I used to do it regularly so I bet him a nickel I could. We switched roles. I waited patiently as the patient copied out the scrambled words for me to work on.

The four words came after some effort.

"What's taking you so long?"

From selected letters in these four a fifth word must be made. It blew my mind.

The clue: "What the bright neurologist had."

The answer: A "Brainstorm."

Mental status: 100%

January 6

The old man complained that he could not get a newspaper to do the day's Jumble. Sympathetic ears. I knew that there were some papers on the floor, and I asked the ward clerk how my friend could buy one.

"I'm sorry, but only semiprivate patients can buy papers. If he's a ward patient have him tell his family to bring one in."

I reflected that this man had never married and his family had been buried. I contemplated my chances of changing hospital policy in this issue. Then I went out and bought him a newspaper.

Two minutes later he returned.

"It's too easy today. It's not worth doing."

Each day since he has asked me to get him a paper, "If it's not too much trouble." It is and it isn't, so I do it. But I feel silly as I trade a paper for a dime in full view of the ward. Two things wrong with it: (a) favoritism and (b) reversal of roles. I'll not be making this mistake again.

A man came in with a stroke that had left him weak

on one side. This was the latest of a series of medical problems—he had not been very lucky. One of the nurses recognized him from an earlier admission.

"It's good to see you again."

Nurse reflects for half a second, and adds, "I hope this is your last time in here."

"So do I," says the patient wearily. "One way or the other, so do I."

January 7

Sometimes I introduce myself as "Doctor" MacNab, sometimes as "mister." I am usually careful about whom I try this on.

Yesterday when I finished examining the stroke patient, he showed that he had some reservations about my abilities.

"You know, I think you're as much of a doctor as I am."

I smiled. (The resident had introduced me that way.)

Today I had studied his chart and in my questioning revealed an intimate knowledge of his previous history. This must have impressed him (although that was not my intent), because at the end he asked, "Doctor, do you think I'll recover?"

I did not know the party line on his prognosis, so I said yes. The chances are good. Of course, there might be some residual weakness (a phrase that covers everything up to paralysis).

"Doctor, I have a car. Do you think I'll ever drive it again?"

I said I was not sure of the laws in this area, but if he stayed as he was he could always have the controls modified. And if he recovered, he was home free.

He thanked me.

The next day he told me he'd had his sister sell the car. $100. Wise man.

I found out later that my "guarded optimism" was in fact the party line. His chances are very good.

January 8

I stopped around to see how this patient was doing. The strength in his arms is beginning to come back.

"Any complaints?"

"Not really. Only I'm beginning to see double."

Catch-22 and the man who saw everything twice. I started to explain why I was smiling but soon gave up.

January 9

The neurosurgery ward is quiet and civilized, like walking into a temple. You feel you should remove your shoes at the elevator door. The postop patients lie with their heads wrapped in large turbans, alert but silent, perhaps wondering if they are still alive. Those whose bandages have been removed reveal completely shaved heads—even the women. Buddhists (or collaborators). There seems to be one nurse for every bed.

I ran into a resident who had been on our floor and was now on neurosurgery. I asked him rhetorically if he liked the switch. Our ward is the most frustrating place I have found in the hospital. All the doctors do is make the diagnosis and decide whether treatment will consist of sending the patient up to the surgeons or sending him out to a nursing home. (There is some pill therapy and this is very gratifying when it works.) The main activity of the doctors and students is pasting results in the chart. I remember the resident working at that task with the gentle patience of a man who is near the end of his sentence. The real work of the ward is taking care of "zonked-out" patients—feeding them, washing them, exercising and turning them over so they don't get bedsores. This is done by the aides, nurses, attendants, and by the physical therapists. We decided that the ward would function better without doctors at all.

A case in point is a patient who developed paraplegia shortly after an operation for a slipped disk (at another hospital, naturally—we see everybody's failures). This guy is one of the failures of the medical profession and he should have gone to a chiropractor or learned to live with his pain. The only thing we can offer him now is physical therapy to teach him how to get around with a wheelchair, and occupational training (he used to work in a steel mill). The longer he sticks around the hospital, the more bad things seem to happen to him. He was getting his medication IV and a phlebitis started in his arm at the IV site. One day later he starts spiking a temperature. I felt this was due to the phlebitis and would go away when his arm got better, but the resident decided to give him "the fever work-up." This consists of culturing the throat and the urine and the blood. Blood cultures are a pain. You have to be careful you do not contaminate your specimens. Furthermore, this guy has one arm out (with phlebitis) and only one vein on the other.

I got one set of blood cultures on him, but this is more than a one-shot process. You have to take specimens over several days. The resident took them the next day, and on the third day it was my turn again. I collected the equipment (which involves running around and looking in closets—nothing is where it should be) and approached his bed.

"Mr. Watson, we're going to have to draw some blood."
"You already took all my blood. Aren't you satisfied?"
"We are going to have to take some more."
"Is it going to help me walk again?"

That stumped me. I did not know if he had been told he would probably be paralyzed for life.

"No, this is to figure out what's causing your fever."

"I'm not worried about no fever. My arm's sore."

I started to formulate a homily on the ravages of any untreated septicemia, but thought better of it. The worst that could happen is that he would die, and he might even prefer this (early paraplegic depression). I knew that if I were a good "doc" I would talk him into cooperating, but I felt as unconvinced as he did.

I told the resident about his refusal, adding that my rhetoric was hampered by my doubts about the importance of these tests (I had never seen a positive one).

The resident said he had two points in response:

(1) Taking blood from someone is not like cutting off his leg. There are almost no contraindications for venipuncture.

(2) There is admittedly only a small chance that the culture will be positive, but the possibility exists. If this hospital were "Podunk General" we would not be drawing these cultures. But this is not "Podunk General."

I thanked the resident for straightening me out and wished him good luck with Watson. (I don't think he ever bothered drawing the blood.)

A few days later the report comes back: four blood cultures grew out yeast. YEAST! Is it true? The four specimens were all taken at the same time, from the same site, by the resident. I say it is contamination. He agrees this is the best explanation, but we have to draw blood cultures for another couple of days to see if there are any more yeasties around. All other cultures negative.

Arm gets better, fever goes away. We stop drawing blood cultures. Verdict: contamination.

Somehow I think this patient might have been better off in "Podunk General." They might have left him alone.

January 12

On new patients we should do a complete physical exam as well as a neurological, usually after the residents have finished theirs. They tend to breeze through the former and concentrate on the latter; with us it is the other way around. The more experienced men tend to describe the physical findings in each area as "normal," often, I suspect, without really checking. On two patients whose genitalia were described "normal ♂" I found a bulging inguinal hernia in one and an undescended testicle in the other. The residents are very good at homing in on the immediate problem, but they can be very sloppy about peripheral ones.

January 13

Gifts were offered today for the first time.

The old man who did the Jumble finally left the hospital. (We had failed to discover anything really out of line after a week of testing.) He was grateful for the attention I had paid him (including the newsboy routine) and he tried to tip me $2 on his way out.

I value my services as a newsboy much higher than that, and I knew he was on Social Security, so I refused him politely, urging him to put it in the second collection. We parted friends.

A distinguished Puerto Rican who used to be a lawyer and now resembled Major —— de Coverley came in today. He speaks only Spanish. I started to ask him questions for the standard medical history, with his son translating for us, but I rapidly decided to copy this from the resident's note. His son had to catch a plane; so after three sentences I thanked the patient for his cooperation and told him I would examine him later. I turned to go, but he stopped me.

"Doctor." He pointed to a shopping bag containing several slim boxes. He pulled one out and handed it to me.

It was obviously going to be a necktie. I'd heard he'd already given one to the attending and the resident. Like tipping the steward at the start of the voyage. Principle dictated that I turn it down. Common sense told me that this patient would be insulted if I refused his gift. Common sense won easily.

It was a much nicer tie than I had expected. I resolved not to wear it while I was on neurology. (The attending wore his the next day.)

January 14

Our attending calls himself "the last of the dodoes" (he practices as neurologist and psychiatrist). He determines whether the patients referred to him have an actual brain tumor or are just "disturbed." A few are both:

"Unfortunately, being crazy does not confer the blessing of immortality."

He is really the last Puritan. He is a tall, youthful-elderly man from the kind of background where men can afford not to compromise their principles. He has clear blue eyes, and his face is frozen in a slight prognathic smile, which he accentuates with emotion. His smile is mechanical when he uses an amusing phrase, but when he discovers we are also amused it is radiant, and this is charming. He stifles it, though, and continues his discourse.

He is a great examiner. When the patient comes in he offers his right hand; they shake; he squeezes and smiles as the patient squeezes back. Then he swings his left hand into shaking position. The patient is surprised, but responds and the playful squeeze is repeated. In these ten seconds he gets a rough estimate of the relative strength of each side of the body. The rest of his examination is similarly efficient. But he is not cold: he compliments the patient even on a poor performance. The patients like being examined by him, whereas they do not like being examined by me.

He has an empathy with the patient which the younger men (including the students) lack. When the residents learn that the X-rays indicate that one of our patients has a brain tumor, they say, "Aha!" as if their hunch paid off. When the doctor learns of the evidence, however, a reflex grimace spreads across his face. He is beyond hunches.

I think he is an example of the final stage of Erik Erikson's "Human Life Cycle"—the stage of "ego integrity versus despair." A friend of mine pointed out that "medicine is an ego trip," i.e., doctors are after fame and/or the chance to play God. This man has gone beyond that: he is of himself—his life has assumed a kind of inevitability in that it could not have been otherwise.

He also has a little trouble with his fly. This keeps him within human proportions.

A very good man.

January 15

One resident asked the attending if a carotid arteriogram should be done on an aged patient who has been zonked out for the past month. X-rays show a mass in his brain, and this procedure would tell us if it were a big clot or a tumor. This test has about a 1% mortality rate, and even if a tumor were demonstrated this man would be a poor risk for surgery. The resident asked if nevertheless the arteriogram should be done for academic interest. He admits to playing devil's advocate.

The attending paused two seconds.

"You can never justify doing anything for academic interest that penetrates the skin of the human body." Smile indicating I'm sorry but that's final.

"What about X-rays?"

"That's different."

Another resident pointed out that what this patient needed was not an arteriogram but a syringe full of morphine. "If there ever was a candidate for euthanasia, he is it." A terrific bull session followed. We started off on euthanasia—most of us were against it, for different reasons. A resident who happens to be Catholic widened the battlefield to include abortion, and found himself alone. He used words like "form," "kind," and "essence," but never mentioned "soul."

Q. When is a human?

He asked the attending to admit that abortion was a form of murder.

"All right, if you want to look at it that way, but that wouldn't stop me."

Would the attending be willing to face these people on Judgment Day? That is, if he believes.

"I am an Episcopalian—very low church. I believe in Judgment Day, and I will be willing to stand up and face everyone."

(You see—the sense of inevitability.)

Continuation of the monologue on forms and essences. I wondered if the resident had ever seen the results of a sloppy criminal abortion. Possibly no.

After an hour the attending apologized and said he had an appointment.

His conclusion: "God save us all."

On with the show.

January 16

Last day in neurology. We ask the attending to give us the pitch.

Q. Is it an overapplied field?
A. No. There are less than 800 Board-certified neurologists in the country, with most of these in the Northeast. Neurosurgery, however, is overapplied—there aren't enough brain tumors to go around.
Q. Doesn't this tend to be a depressing field?
A. Not really. 98% of the people who you work up turn out to be normal, and you are overjoyed to be able to tell them they don't have one of these terrible diseases.

I did my first LP's* today. I have a long way to go.

* Lumbar punctures, or spinal taps.

Psychiatry

January 19

Reading the schedule for the psychiatry rotation is like leafing through a brochure for Bermuda.

The luxury of an 8 o'clock breakfast (and the freedom to carry a morning paper without getting nasty looks from my superiors, who are themselves carrying papers).

No weekend or night duty.

Every other afternoon off.

The Queen of Sciences.

The Harlot of the Arts.

Psychiatry.

Outpatient clinic: Sane people who are poor.

My first patient was a sad young woman with "vague somatic complaints" and problems at home—marital and financial. Yes, sometimes her teeth itched. Because she lives outside our district we can "evaluate" her but not treat her. (Often patients will consider themselves cured after evaluation alone.) We were warned against establishing a "bond" with these patients, but I found this hard to resist. Her troubles were mainly external, and this made her sympathetic. Previously I thought that the only people who went to psychiatrists were people who were slightly nuts. This is a reasonable woman, slightly "depressed." By listening to her for two hours I felt I had done her some good.

This could be a great way to earn a living.

January 20

We were bussed to a state mental hospital this morning. Architecture by engineers—very depressing. I hope I never have to work in such a place.

We were given a lecture on "organic" senile dementias, i.e., those with a physical cause. Two cases, each with an interesting onset: (1) One woman, religious all her life, began to pray aloud at night. (2) A 60-year-old man was noted to increase his activities in buying and selling antiques.

The man feels that his children are Communist agents, and is afraid that the FBI is after them. (This brings out his "paternal concern.") The woman calls the hospital "a home for us all." I hope in my case she is wrong.

I had my first official weekday afternoon off since the start of the third year. I plan to spend all such afternoons studying EKG's for the next rotation, but I squandered this one on a nap.

January 21

I have to hustle in the mornings to be on time for lectures or rounds. Today I hustled to be on time for an appointment with a patient—my housewife with the blues. She was half an hour late. My preceptor urged me to ask her why she was late, to disregard her first answer, and then to ask her THE REAL REASON. I ignored his advice.

This was her second visit, and she was a little more at ease. I asked her some questions I had thought of since the first meeting, and as before she told me more than I wanted to know. It was like trying to turn off a faucet—at first neither direction seems to work. I would nod my head as she answered and make notes, at the same time trying to get direct quotes.

At one point she seemed disturbed by my note-taking. "Does anybody else see those besides the other doctor?" I told her no.

"I'd like this to be confidential. I've never told this to a doctor before."

She proceeded to tell about a violent incident in her life that made the whole case a lot clearer. I stopped taking notes, leaned back in my chair, and tried to put her at ease. A thing like this could happen to anybody. No, it couldn't.

My patient seemed relieved when she was through. She asked me if there was a number she could call if she needed to. She denied suicidal impulses, but felt she might "let go." I was tempted to give her my own number, but we had been cautioned against this and besides I can rarely be reached there. I told her to call the hospital's emergency ward if she wanted help, and this seemed to satisfy her. She has been a clinic patient of this hospital most of her life and has a surprising faith in it. Even though her home is 20 miles away, she comes here for all her problems. Her last four visits here have been for "vague somatic complaints" whose underlying cause escaped detection by examination and laboratory tests.

Spent the afternoon on the phone trying to find a psychiatric clinic nearer her home where she can be listened to for not too much money.

January 22

There is a mental hospital associated with the medical school. I had been to its auditorium and its library, but never its wards. These I penetrated today. My Thursday preceptor (it seems we have one for each day of the week) told me to go to a certain ward and pick up a patient named Bern so he could show us how to conduct a psychiatric interview. I encountered my first locked wards. I had tried the stairs in vain—this one was accessible only by elevator. A single, slow elevator, out of phase with my travels. Frustration mounts. I get to the ward. Teen-agers in ordinary clothes—no hospital pajamas. I ask after a patient named Bern. Nobody has heard of him. An older man who was probably in charge told me there was no patient of that name in the ward. I asked if he could direct me to the nurses' station (or its analogue).

"I am telling you there's no such patient," he said angrily. The patients were looking at me as if I were crazy.

I explained to him that this was a conflict of authorities.

The nurses' station had a list of patients that was only slightly out of date (last month's, with some corrections), and the name Bern was not on it.

I could not exclude the possibility that I *was* crazy. I looked up my preceptor's extension in the hospital phone book, but evidently he was not here when this copy came out three years ago. I called the operator and asked for the extension for Dr. Reinhardt.

"Who's he?"

"He's a psychiatrist."

That clue was no help. I described the location of his office, and the operator set off on foot while I held on.

Two minutes later Dr. Reinhardt identified himself and verified my directions.

"Look, Dr. Reinhardt, if this is some kind of 'stress experience' I surrender."

Dr. Reinhardt was mystified that Bern was not there. He checked his notes, and we went through the ward list for all the permutations his handwriting allowed. No luck.

I got the elevator the hell out of there. We went over interviewing techniques without the assistance of patient Bern. Whatever became of him still leaves me wondering.

I decide I never want to work in one of these places.

Three weekday afternoons on this rotation are spent on "public health." We go down to the municipal hospital in the ghetto (the hospital I used to visit when I was on surgery). We listen to lectures on the problems of providing medical care to the poor. The course was set up in the days when all medical students were aiming at a rich private practice and seems designed to remind them of their "responsibilities." Now a good fraction of my class is interested in going into some form of public medicine, but the course is still as dull as ever. Most of the students "cut" these lectures, and the people giving the course look as if they would like to cut too.

We are assigned patients to work up from the point of view of public health. These patients are guaranteed genuine US Grade A poverty-stricken. They are all on welfare. Their health is usually the least of their worries.

My patient was an attractive young woman with seven children. She was separated from her husband. Her mother had been shot at 46. Her oldest daughter was unmarried and had just had a baby. (This daughter bore the patient's own maiden name, which showed there had been a precedent.) My patient had come to the hospital in a stupor, and claimed she had been drinking.

I found her to be a nice woman who was puzzled about our interest in her household. I explained as best I could; I was deliberately vague. I told her we would be visiting her house next week if that was OK by her. I specified that I did not care how many color TV sets she owns and that we would not be reporting to the welfare agency.

She said it was OK. Puzzled expression remained. This seems to me to be an imposition on her but a fine idea as far as we are concerned. Our interests come first.

There was a spectacular accident as we were leaving the hospital. An open truck with boxes of fruit was parked by the main entrance, with prices marked for quick sale. Suddenly a kerosene heater which had been brought along fell off the truck and spread flaming kerosene along the city street. The men pulled the truck ahead, but they were boxed in by double parkers. The street burned—no car dared it. The crates began to catch fire, but one of the men extinguished them with chunks of snow. He kept saying, "Son of a bitch." A policeman conferred with the driver. I didn't stay for the fire engine.

Things like that just don't happen in my part of town.

January 23

Videotape of a psychiatric interview. We all watched it along with two psychiatrists, who would stop the tape (freezing the image) and ask questions like "What can we say so far?" and "What is he really saying?"

The patient was a very attractive young woman, by her own admission "spoiled and lazy." She was an inpatient. She had been having problems for years, and was seductively at ease in the interview. She said she liked interviewers who "responded" to her. This was a nervous young resident who was trying hard not to respond to her. This was his videotape debut.

Her father had been a psychiatrist, and evidently had not paid enough attention to her as far as she was concerned. She was now forcing the psychiatric community to pay a lot of attention to her. She had done this in the past few years and would continue to do so the rest of her life. In again, out again.

A phenomenal waste of time. Quite provocative for both sides, but otherwise a waste of time.

January 26

My depressed housewife was almost on time today. She was also fairly cheerful. Things were going better at home. She'd had a talk with her husband and he was more sympathetic. This was to be her last session. I had arisen at 5:30 to do my write-up on her, and I found it much easier than a medical history. I wrote up everything but the "Plan of Therapy," which I intended to discuss with her. We could not treat her, but I had found a couple of clinics where she could go for $10 a visit, without a "waiting list."

She said she could not afford them, and besides, she didn't want to take the time out from work. She had missed one promotion already.

"Oh, well. I just thought it would be good to have a doctor you could talk to about your problems at home. But it seems to me you are handling them pretty well on your own."

This concluded, I felt free to step out of my role.

"Just out of curiosity, do you ever read books?"

No, she didn't have the time.

I gave a halfhearted plug about the beneficial effects of bad fiction, and excused myself to present her case to my preceptor.

The head of the clinic and a pretty social worker with a virgin pad of yellow paper were also there. We were going to decide WHAT WAS GOING TO BE DONE. I presented my summary of the case. (Diagnosis: Depressive neurosis. Nonsuicidal. Subacute. Resolving.) The patient did not want further psychiatric treatment, and the indications for this were only marginal.

"Do you think she's cured?" I was asked.

"She might come back in six months with vague somatic complaints" (I love that phrase).

"It sounds to me as if we can do nothing more for her." The chief psychiatrist stood up with resolution. Chalk up another victory for the clinic.

The social worker left with her yellow pad intact.

I went out to tell my patient what we had decided.

"You're cured."

"No more visits?"

"No more visits." She looked relieved. I told her to get in touch with the other clinics if she felt the need.

"But what about my headaches?"

That was, after all, her chief complaint. I told her to return to the emergency room if they ever became really unbearable. In retrospect, this girl would have been an ideal candidate for hypnotherapy.

"Thank you, Dr. MacNab."

"You're welcome. Good luck and God be with you."

This woman still had her headaches, but otherwise I felt she had improved under my care. A total of 9 hours of my time—mostly listening—and yet I felt that I had done something for her that none of my classmates could have done as well.

January 27

Medicine is slowly making me into an obsessive-compulsive. At college I never cared about writing instruments— I used whatever came my way, picking them up and losing them with equal indifference. 19¢ Bics, Eberhard Fabers, Pentels, Scripto Mechanical Pencils—they were all interchangeable. Once to avoid writing a love letter in ball-point I went out and bought an Estabrook with a broad nib. Otherwise I didn't care.

Now I care. I've learned that shirts last longer with a

clear plastic "Pocket Saver," in which is sheathed my armamentarium:

1. An Eveready pocket flashlight (slim size, 2 AA batteries)
2. Two 25¢ Bic Fine Points—one blue for writing notes in charts, the other red for writing down results (e.g., hematocrits)
3. A Cross Mechanical Pencil (for my journal)
4. A KOHINOOR Rapidograph with a #2 point, filled with PELIKAN drawing ink. This is my pride and joy. I use it for drawing cartoons of armadillos when things get monotonous.

If I lost any of these I could not continue to function as a clinical clerk. Or as anything else.

This same compulsiveness is found in the little black notebook which is always at my side. The gift of a drug company, it comes with the following tables:

1. Normal values for blood, stool, urine, and spinal fluid
2. A conversion table for changing grams into ounces, drams, grains
3. Desirable weights for men and women according to height and frame
4. A 2-paged conversion table for centigrade and Fahrenheit. (For doctors who have trouble with the formula $°F = 9°C/5 + 32$.)
5. Latin words and abbreviations (including vin. = vinum)

I myself have added:

1. The weekly schedule of my current rotation
2. An outline of what to do in each of the following emergencies
    a. Cardiac arrest (note time on bed sheet . . .)

b. Gunshot wound
  c. Coma
  d. Head injury
3. An outline of how to record the following routine procedures
  a. Postop check
  b. Lumbar puncture
  c. Reading an X-ray of the abdomen
  d. Visual fields examination
  e. Examination of the functions of the eye
4. Various one-page treatises on different topics, including the work-up for low back pain, the differential diagnosis for appendicitis, and the 8 Ages of Man
5. Random notes—a growing list of one-line "pearls," including
  a. The number of teeth a child should have is equal to his age in months minus 6
  b. A patient who uses the word "spine" has probably been to an osteopath
  c. The hysterical headache is constant, bandlike, and metaphorical
  d. When you palpate an abdomen, observe the eyes for pain

Ideally all this information should be in my head. It is now halfway there.

We spent the morning watching a demonstration of live patients and the afternoon watching videotapes of interviews. Videotapes won.

The "live" patients were exhibiting "depression," which meant they hardly exhibited anything at all. Rigid on the edge of the chair, head down, immobile, eyes on the floor. We were told they had manic episodes; looking at them now this was very hard to believe. They all had suicidal impulses and I could think of no good reason to stop them.

Our preceptor showed us videotapes of "the kind of patient you'll never see in clinic."

"As soon as they start acting like this they get locked up. That's why you'll never see them in clinic."

The first patient was a young man who was staring at the doctor with such smiling, eagle-eyed intensity that we burst into laughter as soon as he came on. Yes, delusions of grandeur. The son of a rabbi, now talking like George Lincoln Rockwell. Our preceptor pointed out that our immediate laughter was indicative of the fact that he was psychotic.

The second patient was a manic-depressive in full manic flight. Nonstop. You wanted to strangle her. This reaction is also diagnostic.

We were told to listen for the characteristic "loosening of associations." You couldn't miss it, but you had to struggle to keep up. It was like trying to follow the thoughts of one L. Bloom.

"The cop on the corner," our preceptor reminded us, "can recognize a gross loosening of associations. It behooves you as physicians to learn to detect the subtler forms of mental illness."

I went this afternoon to visit my real Slum Goddess, the Public Health patient with whom I had set up an appointment. The slum she lived in was in a part of the city diametrically opposed to my own—20 miles there and 20 miles back.

That makes 40 miles.

She wasn't in. They didn't know when to expect her. I was furious. Nobody does that to me. (She did.)

Later, I figure out that she had a perfect right to miss our appointment.

There was nothing in it for her.

January 28

Back safely in clinic. My new patient is young, handsome, and black. Whether he is gifted as well, I wish I knew.

He works days for the telephone company and devotes his evenings to acting. Over the weekend, three days after his first opening, he came into our emergency room in a stupor. A four-dollar bottle of Sominex, empty, in his coat pocket. (Take Sominex tonight and sleep.)

A halfhearted suicide attempt. Why?

The acute problem was interesting: The day before opening night, the author decided to cut 17 pages of script. Not all in one place. Scattered here and there. (This was his first play too.) They walked to the theater reading scripts, but otherwise the opening was OK. The next day the author decides to fire the lead and take the role himself, reading the lines from the script during the performance. He stumbled frequently and my patient (who played opposite) had to ad lib to cover for the author.

It was a memorable performance.

My patient decided to forget it.

There were other problems closer to home that he wanted to forget too. I liked working with this guy. He cared about himself. He was dressed elegantly (including lavender shirt and orange silk scarf at the neck). He had big dreams for the future. (Unrealistically big.) And he was open. I tilted back in my chair and laughed at his account of the birth pangs of his play. Very unprofessional, but I thought it was funny, and that's the reaction he was looking for.

My preceptor came in for a short introductory session. I was glad to see that he laughed too. But much more professionally.

January 29

The patient of the day was a 17-year-old boy whose latent schizophrenia was made patent by psychedelic drugs.

A zombie, on a heavy dosage of thorazine. Handshake like a dead fish. Eyes to match.

(Yes, his father was a psychiatrist.)

I was in the room as a classmate interviewed the patient "cold," i.e., without knowing anything about him. My colleague got hung up on his science-fiction delusions.

"You see, I was radioactive. That's why I came here."

My friend decided to ask him about his childhood. He should have been more specific.

"Tell me about yourself when you were little."

"At three years of age I already controlled the world. I had figured out the answer to the riddle of life."

The interview elicited very little in the way of "hard information." When it was over the patient was led back to his ward. Our preceptor turned to the rest of us.

"What other things would you like to have asked this patient?"

I said I would like to have learned the answer to the riddle of life.

Down at the city hospital this afternoon we were introduced to an "activist" community group—one delightful young man, who said he was a "community organizer," and a half-dozen women of spectacular ordinariness. They started small. Learning that the hospital did not supply toothpaste to patients, and that no visitors meant no toothpaste, they campaigned on this issue and won a change of policy. Next issue was the fact that the patients' food was always delivered cold. Another campaign, another victory. They escalated the war to the technical level on the issue of missing X-rays and charts, which result in a long wait for the patient. The interns had been cursing the staff about this for years, but nothing had been done. This committee worked on it, and the charts and X-rays stopped disappearing. They are now trying to see each patient before discharge to get complaints about medical and nursing care. They will not stop until they are running the hospital.

I say let them. They could hardly do worse than we are doing.

But I expect I will change my tune.

January 30

"Kiddies" again. Child psychiatry.

The chart said he was a 13-year-old boy with a complaint of insomnia. His parents were recently separated.

I was not looking forward to this. Memories of adenoidal youths I had known at prep school whose parents had been recently divorced.

He turned out to be too mature for his age. The separation didn't bother him. But his mother was thinking of returning to Puerto Rico. And that's what was giving him insomnia.

"Why don't you want to go back to Puerto Rico?"

"I'd lose my friends, my schooling, and my job." (He earned $15–$20 a week in a lawyer's office.)

I saw that I was in the holy presence of the American Dream. My patriotic duty was clear.

"I'm on your side in this one."

February 2

My actor friend returned for his second session. New outfit. Pistachio shirt, gold cuff links and neckace. His long, light stride propels him into my "office," a thin room with a desk and chair. I take the chair with arms; he gets the straight one and doesn't seem to mind. We sit at right angles along the sides of the desk (which might otherwise become a symbolic barrier between us).

I immediately relax and tilt back. We had started out with some formality on the first session, but this had vanished as my patient told his tale. About midway in describing what the author had done to the play, he had weighed several euphemisms, and discarded them in favor of the unprintable *mots justes.*

"Hell, I might as well talk natural."

We were both more at ease after that.

This time he was completely relaxed from the start. Hearing him talk about his early childhood was like listening to the Bill Cosby record "I Started Out as a Child." The games he played would be even better night-club material than Cosby's "Street Football." *

Other things not so amusing. Most of the friends of his youth have a "habit." Which means an addiction for heroin. He says he will buy them food, but not give them money. Once he did give a guy money. Two bucks.

"I figure it was better than having him go out and pick up a cop."

His own minor personality problems seem by comparison a bourgeois luxury.

This afternoon in Public Health we had an introduction to a methadone program. I had asked my actor what he thought of this drug, and he said it made the difference between a black, hairy ape on your back and a white, crew-cut one. In other words, he did not think much of methadone.

The people I met this afternoon may have been carefully selected, but they were true believers. One ex-addict with silver crew-cut hair and a cigarette-burn hole in his pants got up and read a speech he had written on three crumpled sheets of lined paper. He used trite phrases like "human individuality," but he talked as if he really meant it, pausing for effect at the end of each earnest period. A man of Great / Natural / Dignity / who was thankful for methadone and looking forward to the day when he could

---

* Erikson, p. 86, *Childhood and Society*, W. W. Norton and Co., 1963: "Observation of primitive societies show acts of intercourse between children of three and four—acts which, to judge from the attendant laughter, are primarily imitation."

do without it. The others seemed happy to live with it. Methadone was mother's milk, and maybe someday they would wean themselves, but only maybe. One other guy had waited six months to get into the program. He could have been accepted earlier, but his wife was an addict and the doctors wanted both of them or neither. This was his twelfth day on methadone.

"Looking at the pictures of what happened to that addict's skin, I feel happy. I feel that I've been saved."

I'm not so sure he's saved yet, but we're both hoping.

February 3

The light at the end of the tunnel.

I sat around with a friend in the fourth-year class discussing various internships. This was Eric Grey, the man who had left his own public relations firm to go to medical school. We both should have been doing something else, but the topic was on his mind because he had just finished his applications and I was eager to listen. Neither of us is sure which field we want to go into, but Eric is thinking of ophthalmology.

Ophthalmology is a "glamour" specialty that has mastered the laws of supply and demand. Ophthalmologists do well. There are very few ophthalmologists. This equitable system is perpetuated by the fact that there are very few residencies in ophthalmology. It is advisable to apply three years in advance for a place in one of these training programs. These residencies do not have many late nights. The office equipment is expensive, but no ophthalmologist has ever gone bankrupt. A license to print money, and you don't have to kill yourself. And the cause is just. He tries to talk me into it—but an uneasy feeling remains.

Saw a documentary about a municipal hospital on TV. One hour of hopeless situations and heroic deeds. We watched the show in the staff rec room of *our* municipal hospital, which looked like the Mayo Clinic in comparison. With us was a second-year resident, who had seen it all a million times before and was barely interested in watching it now. My friend and I had seen it through only once before. We were all mildly amused by the assorted desperate plights (black humor) and glad that the heroics were not our responsibility tonight. When it was over, Eric sat in his chair and shook his head.

"Ophthalmology. There's no question about it."

February 4

The last session with the actor. Yet another costume, but I have the feeling he has depleted his wardrobe. He has decided to quit his role and continue as an understudy.

My preceptor thinks he is a "hysterical personality" and would benefit from further psychotherapy. We had given him a few days to think about it. Today he tells us it is out of the question.

"I can't afford to take off two afternoons a week from my telephone job. I'd be fired. But, say, what do you doctors think is wrong with me that I need to go for psychotherapy?"

That was a good question to which I did not know the answer. I decided to avoid the concept of the hysterical personality. Instead I talked to him about ambition. His problem was an excess of it. Yes, that was the problem. You need ambition to reach the top, but it can make life difficult on the way up. Psychotherapy might help him understand why he had the ambition and also how to live with it.

My preceptor checked in on us. I informed him of the patient's reluctance to continue therapy; we all shook hands and the session broke up.

"You start learning about a patient when you stop asking him questions." S. Freud. Now that these sessions were officially over, the patient took me aside and talked to me about the real problem: his wife. Before, he had told me she was "intelligent, beautiful, but not worldly." He felt he could not talk to her about his acting. She had attended the opening and, I now learned, "watched me make love to another woman for the first time." (I had known they had a fight on the morning of the attempt, and that she had tried to persuade him to quit acting, but this made the whole thing clearer.) He felt the need for a worldlier woman. "If I ever marry again, it won't be a virgin next time." He was thinking about divorce, but was held back by the fact that his wife loved him, was such a fine person, and that her family had been very nice to him. He just couldn't do it.

What to do. I congratulated myself on my bachelor status. I advised him to spend more time with his wife. (For the past three months, he had been home only six hours on the average weekday.) His demotion to understudy meant that free time would be there. He should also introduce her to his world and "worldliness" by taking her to plays and movies. And not waste his money on hit shows and the best seats, or showing off his clothes. But to go and enjoy it and share his enjoyment with his wife.

My friend said he would try it, thanked me, and the elevator swallowed him up. An interesting case. I felt I had been moderately successful: he was now more "realistic" about his ambitions than he had been when he started. But I almost missed the boat on a "major area of conflict." I hope things work out. I have much to learn.

February 5

Never interview a patient on an empty stomach. That was my first mistake. I was late, anxious, and had skipped breakfast. I had to interview a patient before my preceptor and three other students.

My patient had been in the hospital eight months after "flipping out" and threatening to jump off a bridge. I had never seen her and knew nothing about her. The purpose of this exercise was to see how much psychiatric information I could extract in one hour. She was not the only person being examined.

She was an attractive 33-year-old woman with dyed blonde hair. She had grown up in Appalachia, married as soon as she could, moved to California, and raised two children. But her husband had caught her "cheating" and divorced her. She realized "I had lost the man I loved," and turned to alcohol and pills.

I have lately become interested in Country and Western music, because it provides me with a vicarious emotional life. In listening to this woman I was struck by a pattern of living which is one of the main themes of these songs: the luxuriant self-pity surrounding adultery, alcoholism, and leaving home. I spent the rest of the interview filling in the details of this classic portrait: finding out at what age her parents had let her go out on dates (a "strict" 15), how she felt about living in a distant city, etc. I also asked her how she felt now ("Fine") and whether she felt she might make another suicide attempt ("No"). At the end of the hour, I thought the portrait of C & W Woman was reasonably complete in its historical details.

I threw the ball to my preceptor. He looked at her for a while and said, "Tell me what you like about yourself."

The woman seemed to open up. She had spent the last hour filling out my questionnaire, and here was somebody to talk to. She also told what she disliked about herself, and how she "felt about" her husband.

I got the message.

When she had left, the preceptor pointed out that my performance was a typical one for a medical student. I had got down everything except the "dynamic information": I had no data about what kind of person was sitting before me.

I felt I knew her as a stereotype, but I decided not to bring up the topic of Country and Western music. I would have been torn to shreds.

The student who had been assigned to her brought up a piece of "dynamic information" that we had both missed.

Her husband was black. And she was white.

There are some topics that never come up in Country and Western lyrics, for some reason.

February 6

My 13-year-old showed up again, without his mother. He was carrying a newspaper, and read the sports page while he was waiting.

I asked him about his insomnia, the original chief complaint. No more problems; it looked like his mother was not going to take him back to Puerto Rico after all.

Two areas concerned him. First, he was worried about his height. He was now 5 feet 4½ inches, and he was afraid he was not going to grow much taller. He had received "bad nourishment" during his childhood in Puerto Rico. His first year here he had tried to make up for it by drinking two quarts of milk a day. Now he had stabilized at three glasses.

I told him he was just entering the period when he would grow the most. His father was 5 foot 9 and he would easily reach that, I promised.

The other problem was girls. He could not figure out why girls liked him. He liked girls, some better than others. Sometimes when he was with a girl he knew he could do anything he wanted, but he was afraid. Sometimes he stayed up nights wondering what he was going to do the next day about the problem.

Ah, Sigmund, come in and close the door.

A man-to-man talk on sex followed. I was superb. He looked relieved after I had finished. There was only a whiff of the lingering suspicion that his sex life was richer than my own.

Pills.

Pills are easy to get hold of as a medical student. A classmate gave me some mood elevators he had received from a drug-company representative as a free sample. I accepted them out of curiosity and the hope that they might be fun. I rationalized that I might prescribe these someday and should know their effect. I put off taking them because I wanted to wait for "ideal" conditions; i.e., a slight depression that was unrelated to a hangover. These conditions never arose.

I was talking today with another student who had been a paid subject for a pharmaceutical company's testing of this general kind of drug. He said that my pills would not work until I had built up blood levels, i.e., after several days' dosage. The prospect of ingesting anything, even caviar, for several days to build up a blood level was not appealing, so I fed my pills to the wastebasket. (Just for the record, I put marijuana in the same category as Benedictine: on occasion, very nice, after dinner.)

I was in a bar tonight and the topic of psychopharmacology came up once again. My drinking partner was a classmate who is capable and conscientious, and who told me he took LSD on weekends that were free. (It was very important not to have to be doing anything the next day.) He and his roommates had an established medical reputation in the drug underground and were used to getting calls at strange hours to help someone on a "bummer." He would grab some thorazine, head down to the party, but usually found that reassurance and some physical contact were sufficient medicine to bring the person out of his bad trip.

My friend is interested in specializing in this field. I think he would be good at it. I am sure he would enjoy his research.

February 7

I am responsible for working up two patients in the psychiatric service. I am having a tough time seeing them. One patient works outside and we are never free simultaneously; two more patients had already been discharged when I was assigned them.

I finally connected with one today. A 65-year-old man who entered a month ago after his marriage of three weeks had gone on the fritz. Depression, possibly suicidal. Now he appears normal, except for one obsession. He wants to get out. He wants to get out. He wants to get out.

"You will get out, sir, when you are cured."

"But I feel fine. Listen, can you help me get out of here?"

I told him I would speak to his doctor about it. Somewhere along the line I have learned how to lie.

Later I asked the Viennese nurse why we don't let him out.

"He has nowhere to go."

I point out that he has an apartment and an enviable pension.

"Ah, but you see, you can't have him living alone. He might kill himself."

I suggest that maybe he has a right to do so.

"I agree with you on that, but you are in the wrong profession. The hypocritic (sic) oath says that you should save people. You are only a student now, but someday you will have to take that oath."

I suggest that maybe I can cross my fingers when I come to that part, but she doesn't get the point. I ask her what profession I should be in.

She eyes me up and down.

"Banking."

I still needed another patient. As I was leaving, I noticed a good-looking girl sitting down at the other end of the hall. She looked up and smiled. It is often hard to tell the patients from the staff in this part of the hospital, but she was reading a magazine with such indolence that I knew she had to be a patient. Quick decision: should I go see the departmental secretary on Monday and get assigned another patient who has just been discharged, or should I make my own selection now. She was so attractive, I just could not let this opportunity pass.

"Excuse me. Would you be free now for an interview?"

She put down her magazine and looked up.

"Why me?"

"Why not?"

She did not respond to that at all. I will be looking for a new assignment next week.

February 9

On psychiatric emergency.

I took part in my first miracle cure.

A thirtyish lady of Latin extraction had come in for a regular clinic appointment in another part of the hospital and was unable to leave because of a sudden paralysis of her legs. She had been followed in clinic because of seizures and "shakes" of possible psychiatric origin.

I arrived as the resident was presenting the case to the senior psychiatrist on duty. The diagnosis was conversion hysteria. The patient was angry at her husband because he had not come home this weekend. Why her anger had assumed this form was a matter for speculation: maybe her paralysis would prevent her husband from abandoning her, maybe it was the result of a repressed desire to kick his rear end all over the block. The resident said he planned to "cure" her with an injection of saline. He had found this effective in previous situations.

The older man agreed that this would work for now, but advised against it: to pretend to treat this as if it were something "real" would only complicate later psychotherapy. It would be better to do nothing except to tell her she was all right, that she could walk, but that she might have a slight limp. This last idea was to leave her an out.

We went in to see her. A fat, plain woman sitting in a wheelchair—I didn't blame the husband for taking the weekend off. Her arms and upper trunk would jerk every three seconds unless she was coughing. She showed the classic sign of "la belle indifference"—she seemed to accept these spasms as if they were no more than a tic. Every so often she made a dab at her eyes with a handkerchief.

Her husband was with her, and also a friend. The psychiatrist suggested that there was nothing physically wrong with her. She continued to jerk.

"My wife don't need a psychiatrist." (JERK JERK) "I took her to a specialist in Puerto Rico who say she 100% right in the head." (JERK JERK)

We would see about that later. The immediate problem was to get her out of the hospital, into the cab, and up five flights of stairs to her apartment. We tried to stand her up. She rose from her chair reluctantly. We let go of her arms. She looked as if she was OK, but her knees began to wobble and knock. She watched them helplessly, then collapsed back in her wheelchair and resumed her jerks. More dabs at her eyes with the handkerchief. We were ready to go for the horse needle of saline and to hell with the psychiatry. The kid saved the day.

"This could call for Ace bandages."

The other two agreed that perhaps Ace bandages were indicated here.

"I'll go get some from surgery."

I returned with two new rolls and gave them to the other two to apply. The resident and the psychiatrist each took an elephantine limb and began to wrap the elastic bandage around it. They tried to appear concerned about doing this procedure right.

I felt it was important to imbue these bandages with some magic.

"Remember, take these off as soon as you get to your apartment."

"Yes," the psychiatrist added. "These are only for walking and climbing stairs."

"Whatever you do," said the resident, "don't leave these on at night."

With the bandages secured by a metal butterfly, and the proper incantations uttered, we asked her to see if she could walk now. She might still have a limp.

It must have been a miracle.

We held our breath until the trio disappeared through the front door, and then we broke for dinner.

February 10

I requested and received a new assignment for a psychiatric inpatient.

"This one is not going to be discharged on you. She is really screwed up, and she's going to be here a long time."

I took the elevator to the locked ward and asked a patient where I might find Judy Buckley. He shouted out her name, to my embarrassment.

A striking-looking girl approached me, to my further embarrassment. I had seen her somewhere before. In med school? College? The videotape. This was the beautiful seductive patient whose interview had been shown to us some weeks before.

"What are you smiling at?" she asked me.

"Nothing. I'm John MacNab, third-year student, and I'd like to know if you're free now for a short discussion."

"Oh good, a medical student! They were saying I might get one."

I led her down the hall to an office which luckily or unluckily had glass walls. She was fun to talk to. She was relaxed, open, and had an author's interest in her illness. After all, she had invented it.

Her seductive approach never extended beyond batting her eyelashes, but it made its presence felt. The only thing wrong was her lack of discrimination. She was only interested in me as a medical student or as a person in pants. She wasn't interested in seducing me as ME. That meant that she was really sick.

February 11

The three main "dynamic areas" as defined by my preceptor are (1) aggression vs. passivity, (2) independence vs. dependence, (3) sex.

I am learning that No. 3 is often foremost in the patient's mind when he seeks psychiatric help.

Mrs. Perez, a fortyish mother of two, had a chief complaint of "nerves," but we soon got down to more interesting topics. The main problem was the specter of menopause and the feeling that her sexual life up to now had been unsatisfactory. She had heard other women talk about finding pleasure in "relations," and she felt she had missed something.

I said that we would try to help her in this area, eyeing the stubble on her legs. Would she like to talk more about it next time? I felt I was not prepared to discuss the human sexual response, female, quite yet. Not on the first date.

We did go into her sexual history, which allowed me to relax in the role of "clinical clerk." I felt that the origin of her hangup was grounded in guilt about (a) an attempted rape by her stepfather at the age of 7, (b) an induced abortion and voluntary sterilization.

She was a Catholic. She had not been to church since her marriage, but recently her husband had suggested that they both return to the communion (for business reasons?). This involved going to confession, and she was afraid of what her local priest would say.

It seemed to me that religious anxiety played a large part in her "nerves." I went and asked the clinic secretaries (who all turned out to be Catholic) if they knew of a church with lenient confessors. They gave me two addresses, and I passed these on to Mrs. Perez, with the recommendation to think about going to confession this Saturday. Mrs. Perez was grateful, and it will be interesting to see if her "nerves" disappear. The medieval approach to psychotherapy may be all that is needed here.

February 12

My new social service patient is guaranteed not to fink out on any appointments: she will be confined to the hospital for a month. She is much more cooperative than the former one, but she is also much sicker: she has a heart condition at 35 that may prevent her from seeing 40. Disorganization is the key to her character and fate. We can't even get her name straight; it is down on the charts as Alice Williams, but the Welfare Department knows her as Alice Prescott. No husband. Two children: one 6 years old and not yet in school because his mother has never been able to coordinate the required inoculations; the other was born two months ago and precipitated his mother's heart failure. These children are her main worry: she is afraid that they will be taken away from her because of her disease. They were staying with a niece, but that arrangement will end shortly because the niece wants to go back to work. My job is to find someone to take care of them until the mother can leave the hospital. I have one week to do it.

I tried to solve the problem on a personal basis first. "Is there anyone else who could take care of them, anyone at all?" Yes, maybe; there was a friend on her block, Miss Louise Wood, who might be able to. One thing, though. Miss Wood was 70 years old.

"Is she a young 70 or an old 70?"

A middle-aged 70. Well, we would call her and see. Miss Wood sounded like a young 70 on the phone, or at least a spry one. She asked for a day to think it over. I called her back the next day. She regretted on the grounds that she was just too old. I thanked her anyway.

That meant I had to make a frontal assault on the Welfare Department. I called the number of my patient's case worker, and introduced myself as *Dr.* John MacNab and was immediately glad of the impersonation. The case worker was not in, but would I like to speak to the supervisor. I would indeed. Could I hang on? Yes I could.

I held on for 27 minutes by the clock and several pages of armadillos. If I had introduced myself as John MacNab, third-year medical student, I would probably be waiting now. The supervisor was good to talk to; it was like hearing the voice of the Messiah after 27 minutes of office background noise. I repeated the Dr. MacNab for good measure, and overstated the case. He sounded sympathetic, and suggested we get a full-time housekeeper to live in Miss Williams/Prescott's apartment and take care of the kids. Could we get one on such short notice? He said he'd try.

Later I called him up to ask him about his progress. To my surprise, he said the deal was on. A homemaker will be at the apartment on Monday. The kids will have to be there in the morning.

I called the niece who is currently taking care of them and told her that deliverance was at hand if she could deliver the kids. The niece was disappointed that she would have them over the weekend, and that she had yet to be paid for her services. I guaranteed her remuneration, even if it meant stealing my patient's welfare check and forging her name. But the kids had to be in the right place for the transfer, or else the whole thing would fall through.

"You know the Welfare Department."

She knew.

I wonder if it will come true.

February 13

The source of my 13-year-old's anxiety continues to elude me. Before I met him I felt that everything would be explained by his parents' divorce. After his first visit, I thought it was the fear of going back to Puerto Rico. Last time it was puberty and sex. This time I switched my diagnosis to identity crisis, racial confusion. He told me he was worried about whether he was white or black or "Spanish." His friends were black and he went out with black girls, but his mother preferred his society to be Latin. He felt he was "not qualified for white."

I thought it was better for him to talk to me about these feelings than for me to talk him out of them. When I had learned enough to judge this area to be the *primum mobile* of his unease, I drew him a picture:

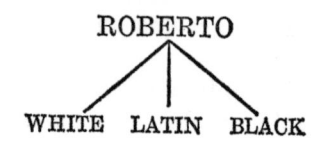

```
            ROBERTO
           /   |   \
       WHITE LATIN BLACK
```

I gave him the 3 x 5 card and explained that he saw himself at the fork. He looked at it with curiosity.

My preceptor had to interview Roberto to get an idea of the case. I gave him my latest interpretation, which he called "very interesting."

"I am sure you are right, but I have to check it out for myself."

A good thing he checked. He came up with a *primum mobile* that was more interesting than any of mine.

WITCHCRAFT.

The woman now living with his father "is a witch." His mother took up the subject after the separation "for protection." Ceremonies include lighting candles under the bed and kicking a coconut around the apartment while smoking a big cigar and muttering things about her former husband. On a small altar is a plate with lettuce, blood, and ashes. Not ketchup, blood.

Roberto says he can't get to sleep at night because he is scared. He is also worried about the bed catching fire.

When he leaves, I apologize for not picking this up in my previous three interviews. My preceptor says it could happen to anybody. He recommends that I get the mother to come next time. I call her up at work, and she says she will come.

February 16

First, a pleasant surprise: the Welfare Department came through. I learned by telephone that the homemaker picked up Miss Williams/Prescott's kids.

Mrs. Perez decided not to go to confession. She admits that religious concerns triggered her depression three years ago, but claims they are not so important now. Even if she did make a good confession she would still be troubled by "nerves." She thinks that her problems have more to do with sex and her lack of pleasure therein.

I ask her if she ever read a novel or saw a movie that touched on this topic.

No. Only "good" movies and books.

Did she think she might enjoy the other kind?

Maybe. Yes.

I later asked my preceptor about this approach to treatment. He flipped me a newspaper and asked me to find a movie that I would recommend. I was unsuccessful. Anyway, movies idealize sex: What is needed are films of ordinary middle-aged couples making love. My preceptor also pointed out that any therapy for this patient would have to include her husband. It was not much good her doing these things on her own.

I told Mrs. Perez I would see her next week.

In the emergency room I tagged along behind the resident and saw:

(1) A 16-year-old girl who looked 30 and had tried to end it all by swallowing an overdose of an antibiotic and sodium bicarbonate. None too bright. Her mother had enough sense to go to the drugstore and ask for something that would induce vomiting. The druggist prescribed syrup of ipecac and it worked. When she came in she was more a psychiatric problem than a medical one: she was awake, hunched over in a chair, depressed and unresponsive to our questions.

(2) A 56-year-old woman who looked 30, thanks to some facial surgery. She now felt that the plastic surgeons had tried to destroy her. She was being followed by a psychiatrist here, and tonight her paranoia was getting out of control.

In both cases I got the feeling that the patient did not want me around and so I walked out of the interviews. This is the man's work of psychiatry: the resident has to decide whether these people will try to kill themselves and whether they should be locked up that night. They asked my opinion, and I said I didn't think so, but I'd hate to be wrong.

February 17

We took a bus trip to view what a classmate called "ONE OF THE WORLD'S FINEST PRIVATE COLLECTIONS" (OF PEOPLE).

It was a visit to a state hospital for the mentally retarded, and my roommate urged me not to go. ("It's just disgusting.") I went because I didn't want to go.

The place reminded me of a New England preparatory school because of its one-story stone buildings in a country setting. Also because it was miserable. The kindly old German doctor who was in charge showed us around. He first gave us a lecture on the various causes of mental retardation, and illustrated each kind with a magnificent specimen from the collection. Chromosomal Defects, Congenital Rubella, RH Incompatibility, Lead Poisoning, Schizophrenic Autism. Some were nice, like the microcephalic who looked like a David Levine cartoon. The saddest was a girl who in playing had made a pie and used lead paint for the icing. She was in a straitjacket to keep her from self-mutilation. With her you got the feeling that the Christian act would be an overdose of morphine.

We were shown two cottages. The "high-grade" one was for patients with IQ's of 30–50. That was fairly civilized: the children were lining up to go for a walk. A tribe of mongoloids is an unusual sight: they are all friendly.

The next cottage was a zoo. One room had 50 shrieking girls, some naked, some sitting, some fingering themselves, some dancing, some taking our arms as we walked through. A nurse waited with a mop, and the floor was sticky from urine. Another room of 50 caged beds, each with a child inside. The shrieks are quieter here. We talk with one 8-year-old whose bones have not grown beyond infancy. She spends a lot of time looking at the ceiling. A color TV in the corner broadcasts a quiz show.

Q. Which of the following has the longest tail, a tapir, a wart hog, or a wildebeest?

But nobody is looking at the idiot box.
"How long do they live like this?" the doctor in charge is asked.
"I'm a neuropathologist, and I like to examine the brains. But they never die. They never die."
I come out of the building with relief; the air tasted clean. My roommate was right—it was a grim experience, and I was not obligated to go, but I think this *should* be one of the requirements for becoming a doctor.

February 18

Since this was to be her last session, I asked Mrs. Perez what she wanted in the way of further treatment. She said that she had come here because she was uneasy about discussing "certain topics" with the psychiatrists back in Puerto Rico. She felt freer with me, and in the course of our sessions "had got a lot off her chest." Some chest.
I told her that she was basically sound, but she did have *"problemas,"* and might feel the need to talk to a doctor from time to time. Right now it made sense for her to return to Puerto Rico. She agreed. While she waited I went up to the departmental office and checked out the directory of the American Psychiatric Association. There were four members listed in her hometown. One of these she had been to before and was a family friend. He was out. I looked up the *curricula vitae* of the other three, found them adequate if not impressive, and made out a list.
She liked the one with the Anglo-Saxon name.

Goodbye and good luck.
"Are you going into psychiatry, Dr. MacNab?" the secretary asked me as I turned in the chart.
"I am not sure. Do you think I should?"
"Yes."
"Do you think everybody should?"
"No."
Very gratifying.

February 19

My beautiful psychiatric inpatient was subjected to a stress interview. It was supposed to be an ordinary interview in the presence of our preceptor group, but Franklin the martinet did the interviewing, and it was a stress interview. Machine-gun questions. I kept quiet and did not interrupt, that was the deal, and he had kept quiet during my interview. But it was torture.

Franklin had himself come under fire last week. They had shown us a taped interview with a hostile 15-year-old boy, and asked how we reacted to the patient. I said I disliked him because he was a punk. Franklin said he had no emotional reaction, and that an interviewer was not supposed to have one. (I asked if Franklin had any emotions, which is a question I have been thinking about since I first met him, but this was ignored.) The psychiatrists took Franklin to task for not sensing or not admitting his reaction, and not taking it into account in his evaluation of the patient.

He certainly did not appear "neutral" today. He was cold and aggressive in his questioning, and the girl read this as hostile. Again, the preceptor bailed her out after an hour. By hesitating for a few seconds before he came out with the soft-spoken question, he communicated that HE UNDERSTOOD.

She was still glad to get out of there. "That was murder. I was going to have an interview with another medical student who asked me yesterday, but I think I'll cancel it. I'm getting tired of exposing myself."

When I had dropped her off and returned to my group, the preceptor was telling Franklin about the need to SHIFT GEARS.

"The mile-a-minute technique may work in physical medicine. It doesn't work in psychiatry, and I don't even think it works in physical medicine."

Franklin replied that he had to get all the information he could because this was a diagnostic and not a therapeutic interview.

"Every interview is a therapeutic interview," our preceptor corrected him.

However, if this girl no longer is compelled to expose herself, then Franklin's technique just might be considered therapeutic!

February 20

Roberto told me some more about voodoo. He explained that there were two kinds: a good kind which could save people and protect them from spells, and a bad kind which could cast spells. He only believed in the good kind. His mother's mother had special powers, but "she worked for God." His mother had always been interested in the subject and had resumed this hobby when her husband had left her. She kept her altar candles burning all the time and only did "special things" on Friday night. Roberto said this didn't bother him so much now, as she always locked the door when she worshipped.

His mother had come today too. A dark, attractive woman who spoke little English. She handed me a note.

To Whom It May Concern
Mrs. Sylvia Constanza

COMPLAINS THAT HER SON ROBERTO HIS BEHAVIOR IS NOT IMPROVED AND CAUSED HER TO MUCH CONFUSION, HE IS HAVING ARGUMENT WITH EVERYBODY AT HOME. SHE REQUESTED IS POSSIBLE TO TAKE HIM INTO THE HOSPITAL FOR TREATMENT. PLEASE, TAKE CARE THE CHILD AND MOTHER'S PROBLEMS AS SOON AS POSSIBLE

If anybody should be in the hospital, I was sure it was not Roberto.

My preceptor and I tried to interview the mother, but the language barrier was too high to cross. The hospital interpreters were busy, so I went over to prenatal clinic and found a patient who could translate for us. (She was superb.) We asked Mrs. Constanza about the things that were troubling her. Paroxysmal headaches and chest pain. I wanted to find out about witchcraft and resolved on an indirect approach. Was she afraid the other woman was trying to hurt her? Yes. How? A shrug of the shoulders. Did she believe in witchcraft? No. There were two kinds: one good, the other bad. Did she believe in the good kind? Well, yes.

She finally admitted that she knew of the other woman's spell to hurt her and her children. (This spell was probably the source of her painful attacks.) We never questioned her about her own activities in this field; we felt our suspicions were justified. She asked us if she might be able to see a psychiatrist. We said that we would help to arrange it.

I gave her my report on Roberto. Roberto was a good boy who was trying to become a man. He resented his mother's attempts to control his life. She should not worry about his friends, because he was not the kind to abuse drugs. And she should let him select his own clothes, for after all he earned the money to pay for them.

Even with an interpreter, I doubt if any of it sunk in.

I had a session with Roberto, and we talked about his plans to become an airline pilot. I tried to steer him toward aviation mechanics, which would be more realistic, but Roberto was pretty sure he wanted to be a pilot. I told him that money would promote this ambition, and he should save some of the money he now spent on clothes.

Roberto asked if he could come next week. There was no child psychiatry clinic, but I would be free at the time, and I felt he wanted to talk some more.

My preceptor said this was a very interesting case. He suggested that our difficulty in finding out what was wrong with Roberto could be explained by the theory that there was nothing wrong with him, and that his mother had brought him in to bring herself closer to help.

February 23

Because today was a holiday, I had to work. In the chemistry lab. I was not on duty, but I knew that the guy who was would get inundated and I volunteered to back him up. We were both swamped. There was only one good thing about it. This was my last day AND I AM NEVER GOING TO WORK AGAIN.

If the bank approves my application for a loan.

February 25

We were shown the videotape of a patient and asked to make a diagnosis. The man reminded me of a taxicab driver: he talked a lot, had strong opinions, and was a bore. He said that he had spent the last six months lying in bed and drinking. He worried about his body: he felt his face could swell up in a matter of seconds.

What's your diagnosis?

We had an argument about whether this facial swelling was a delusion or a hypochondriacal complaint. That was the crux between a diagnosis of "schizophrenia" and one of "a hysterical personality disorder."

"We showed this tape to groups of doctors on both sides of the Atlantic," our preceptor told us. "In England they say it is a personality disorder; here they generally say it is schizophrenia. The diagnosis makes a difference in terms of treatment. Here they would lock him up; in England they would treat him as an outpatient. My personal feeling is that both approaches are doomed to failure, but patients are better off outside the hospital. Unfortunately he was hospitalized four years ago; he thinks of his institution as home, and I doubt that he will ever make it on the outside now."

So you see, psychiatrists are not infallible.

February 26

We delivered our reports in public health. I threw away the recommended outline and just said what we had been able to do for the patient. It went over well, but I knew that this was only one small part of my patient's disorganized life. I may get an honor grade for what I have done, but there is much more to do. And I feel guilty about not doing it.

A classmate asked me to go along with him to visit his patient in a tough neighborhood. He was going to bring him some kitchen utensils—a frying pan and a fork—which this patient was currently lacking. We walked ten blocks to the apartment and found he was not at home. There was nobody we could leave the stuff with. We caught the next bus home. My friend apologized, but I thanked him for setting up the perfect ending for public health.

I finish this rotation with a feeling of having solved

some problems in a way that would someday justify a salary of $6000 a year.

Satisfaction.

February 27

Saw Roberto this morning and talked with him about becoming an airline pilot. This is something I know about because I have neighbors who are and a brother who wants to be. I had called his guidance counselor at school and learned that he was a bright, well-behaved boy. (This I would have predicted.) He would have no trouble getting into a technical aviation high school, but the counselor recommended taking an "academic" course and going to college. I plugged this, and told Roberto to save his money to buy flying lessons. But he was preoccupied: his mother and the other woman nearly had a fight the day before, and he was worried.

"Are you afraid that your mother might lose her mind?"

"Yes."

I told Roberto about my problems in finding what was worrying him and my suspicion that there was nothing wrong with him at all. Who had decided that he had trouble getting to sleep?

"My mother. She made me come in."

I wrote a note to his mother recommending that she come in soon for another "talk," and I also got her chart from the record room and wrote a full page about what I had learned, with the recommendation that she be sent directly to a psychiatrist the next time she came through our doors.

Writing the report on Roberto's problem will be mechanical. I'm sorry I took so long to get down to the real problem, but it was nice knowing him.

Medicine

March 1

"The medicine rotation isn't as bad as it's made out to be," my roommate advised me. (He had just finished this service.) "It's worse."

I had my second nightmare about it last night. In each case the theme is that my incompetence is detected.

Here goes.

March 2

The inevitable orientation meeting. I get to meet the other half of my rotation: the people who did neuro when we did psych, and vice versa. I have not been in the same classroom with these people since last May.

Out of eight people in my newly assigned ward group, six have been with me all along. But otherwise I lucked out. No Franklin. All capable, responsible guys (including the subdued Pancho Villa). A good team. Someone points out we will all hate each other in a fortnight.

We also lucked out on the ward. The head nurse is my roommate's girlfriend; the resident is a nice-looking girl with fantastic smoked glasses; one attending is my own physician (he is head of the student health program), and one of the interns is an old drinking companion of mine. This could even be fun.

The patients here tend to be old. On rounds, after hearing the catalogue of their afflictions, you are tempted to question the immediate goal of therapy. I saw one patient who was hooked up to a respirator, EKG machine, urine bag, blood pressure gauge, and an EEG. The last machine had twelve leads hooked up to her scalp, and as the paper ran the pens were marking straight furrows instead of waves. That meant they could turn off the machines.

The main work of the first day is learning about the patients that are "given" to you. I have three, and I spent the evening making up a 3 x 5 card full of data on each. Because I was around, I was given some errands to do: starting IV's and finding some X-rays. Luckily I was not on duty so I got to leave the hospital at 11 o'clock.

Home to a medical journal and a quart of ginger ale. This is not a bad nonlife.

March 3

Of my three patients, two were in relatively good condition. One was a disappointed young woman who had a serious problem with alcohol. She had been on a regimen of special medication to make the merest sip of liquor result in an unpleasant reaction. In spite of this regimen she had downed a fifth of vodka one night last week. This resulted in an extremely unpleasant reaction, and she came to the hospital in a coma. She was now "all better," except she still hated herself. A psychiatric problem rather than a medical one, and she would be treated accordingly. I told her she had enough spunk to do anything she wanted; if she made up her mind to quit drinking she could do it. She said she hoped so.

"One thing for sure. I'm never going to touch those pills again."

The second woman reminded me of Mrs. Portnoy. She had a "fever of unknown origin" for a month and we were still "working her up."

"I'm here over a week now and still you doctors haven't come up with anything. A life of sacrifice, and now I'm falling apart. I tell you, I'm falling apart."

It is tough to escape from this woman.

On my way out I meet her son. Fine boy. Dressed like the Assistant Commissioner.

"Tell me, doctor, is this something serious?"

I tell him that her tests so far have been normal, and that the most likely diagnosis at this point would be arthritis.

"That's a relief." A nervous smile.

I can appreciate his disappointment.

Mrs. Darby is really sick. She entered a couple of days ago severely dehydrated, lethargic, and with her diabetes out of control. We sensed that something funny was going on inside her, but first we had to stabilize her condition and then proceed with our work-up.

"She needs a unit of blood," the intern told me. "Can you transfuse her?"

I replied that I had never done a transfusion before. Mild annoyance.

"Start an IV, get the blood, and call me when you're ready."

I couldn't even start the IV. This woman's veins were nearly collapsed—she was close to shock.

The intern was doubly annoyed. He started the IV while I fetched the blood. He was careful to check the blood type in the patient's chart and on the dark packet we were about to give her. I watched him set up the plumbing, which is fairly complicated.

"Now you're an expert. I generally stick around for five minutes to see if there's a transfusion reaction. Tell the nurse how fast you want to run it in."

He waddled off, leaving the "expert" to watch out for a transfusion reaction. There was none.

A public lecture on one aspect of medical research rounded out the day. The work is exotic (it deals with enzyme inhibitors) and the conclusions are only tentative. I tried to think of something I had come across that might help and drew a blank. The lecture lasted an hour and a half. I looked around at the attending staff in the audience, who sat in mummified silence, and decided that if I wanted to go into academic medicine I would have to become a lot more interested in enzyme inhibitors. Or even enzymes.

March 4

The patois reduces our titles to monosyllables. In place of "The Attending," "The Resident," "The Intern," and "The Student," we use the terms "The Ding," "The Res," "The Tern," and "The Stud." I like my title best.

There are a variety of terms for patients:

1. *A crock*—a patient with many complaints and no pathology. I suspect Mrs. Portnoy may fit in this category. In private practice, I am told, there is a saying that "The later the phone call, the bigger the crock."

2. *A troll*—an older patient with some innate charm. First applied to alcoholics who are found under a bridge and brought in stuporous and edentulous. They usually claim they are perfectly fine. Trolls are fun.

3. *A turkey*—the turkey is a proud bird who is unaware of his ridiculous appearance. This term can be applied to any patient you think would benefit from a therapeutic pie in the face. The term is also used with some of the

sense of "crock." Outside the hospital, a universal noun, adjective, or verb with a mildly negative connotation.

4. *A gomer*—a nice old man.

Life on this ward is even more frustrating than in neuro. Things are just as hard to find, patients' problems more distressingly acute, and the squawk box is going all the time and loudly. The noise level is debilitating. To study a chart I have to lock myself into a storeroom. I suppose that doctors must have fast communications, but this system is absurd. Every minute of the workday the announcer reads off a list of a dozen or so doctors or medical students (paged as "doctors") whom somebody wants to talk to. Only an occasional "Pete the barber, Pete the barber," or "Special Officer Perez" relieves the tedium. (And I am told that they once paged "Dr. Kant, Dr. Immanuel Kant.") But for the most part it is nightmarish and I look forward to the day when we all have pocket beepers. Including Pete the barber and Special Officer Perez.

March 5

I was told yesterday that I would have to "present" one of my patients (Mrs. Portnoy) for attending rounds. This woman had seven previous admissions and her chart ran to three volumes. Fortunately, though, our lovely and capable resident had written a succinct one-page summary of her past and present problems. This I committed to memory.

My presentation went well. The attending would stop me after each memorized sentence and ask one of my classmates, "What disease does this make us think of?" The patient was down getting X-rays, so my physical findings went unchallenged. I got off easy.

"I think this lady has what has been called 'palindromic arthritis,'" the attending intoned.

"Do we have a Greek scholar among us?"

I raised my hand, because I saw it coming.

"Dr. MacNab. So much the better. Could you tell us what 'palindromic' means?"

"It comes from roots meaning 'running again,'" I replied.

"Yes. Last year we had an English fellow who tried to tell me it had something to do with the hump of a dromedary camel. I looked the word up, and the dictionary agrees with your derivation: 'running again, or recurrent.'"

"I know sir. I wrote it."

This last bit of mischief went right by the attending, who began to discourse on the recurrent nature of this disease. I was playing to the gallery, though, and the interns were choking with glee. Afterward I was praised for "meeting pomposity with pomposity."

I have come a long way since my first presentation.

I was on duty tonight and it was hell. Mrs. Darby has been vomiting a dark green fluid which tests positive for blood. She came in with a high white count, and one of the possible diagnoses was a form of leukemia. Bone marrow studies were done, and the enzymes in her white blood cells were tested. When you hear hoofbeats look for zebras. It now looks as if her problem is a surgical one.

We are trying to get the surgeons to take her off our hands. Her symptoms are those of obstruction, but her X-rays do not back this up. A surgical resident wants to do an exploratory operation, but his attending says she is too poor a risk, and we should stick with "conservative measures."

"Conservative measures" means a lot of work for me. Every time I turn around there is another blood sample to be drawn or another X-ray to be picked up. What I do is called "scut work"—the work that the intern would have to do himself if he didn't have a student to do it for him. When you are on at night you and your partner do the scut work for the whole ward, including those patients in the isolation unit and the intensive care unit.

They ran us ragged. I decided I was in the wrong profession, because I resent sick people, at least old sick people, and tonight I wish they would die.

I got to sleep in an office in the interval between one blood test at 3:30 AM and another one at 5.

This stinks.

March 6

I got my first admission. A classic case of pulmonary tuberculosis. I am very pleased.

The patient is not at all pleased. She insists that she does not have this and, between paroxysms of coughing, maintains that she is perfectly fine. She is a 25-year-old girl who came from Antigua two years ago and retains a calypso personality. No, she never came in contact with anyone who had this disease.

The reason why we are being so tiresome about tuberculosis is the finding of a classic picture on X-ray, a cavity in one lung the size of a baseball, and a positive skin test.

We have to show the presence of the bug for conclusive proof. The intern, my friend, has me make slides of the sputum with a Ziehl-Neelsen stain. I spend an hour looking for "red snappers" (*Mycobacterium tuberculosis*) but in vain. My stains do not quite come out right. Later, I learn that the bacteriology lab has a fluorescent stain that has never missed. I point this out to the intern.

"Oh, it's so much more fun when you find them yourself."

Mrs. Darby looks worse. She had a stomach tube down to drain the liquid, but she vomited again anyway. That means that the stomach tube is not functioning well. We are still in the dark about what is going on inside this lady.

With the help of an attendant I take her to get another set of X-rays. She cannot sit up unaided, so I have to hold her while they take the shots. They give me a lead apron for protection. She stares into the beam with a determined look on her chimpanzee face. She is determined to die.

The surgeons come around to look at this latest set of X-rays, which we examine on a view box in the visitors' room. There are still no definite signs of obstruction. The resident is more eager to "explore" her, and the attending is less reluctant. They compromise: we will continue with "conservative measures," but if her symptoms worsen, at night, the resident can operate.

I thought that she would probably go up to the OR as soon as the attending left the hospital to go home. I left my phone number with the nurses and went home to get a few hours' sleep.

March 7

Mrs. Darby was not operated on last night, but she was scheduled for the afternoon. Went up to look in on it. I started out behind the anesthetist, but the intern who was holding retractors had to leave so I "scrubbed in" as his substitute.

It turns out that Mrs. Darby had good reason to be feeling out of sorts. She had a huge retroperitoneal abscess. Her abdominal cavity resembled an Irish stew: a thick brown gravy covered everything, and an occasional bit of meat could be found floating free.

It looked as if this stew had been in preparation for weeks. The attending must have felt stupid for not operating earlier, so he took it out on the resident and criticized his suturing technique.

Technique on this lady was purely academic. They did their best, however. I admired their courage.

"Let's attack one thing at a time."

They snipped here and sewed there, working as if she had a good prospect of life ahead of her. They restored her GI tract. I held retractors and watched.

"This woman's case has been mismanaged from the start."

Amen.

March 9

Mrs. Darby is alive and not doing so well. It is felt she will not be leaving the recovery room.

The calypso girl with suspected TB is difficult to work up. In the first place, she is in isolation, which means I have to put on a mask and a gown every time I want to see her. Anything I bring out of the room must be left under ultraviolet light for 10 minutes, and a sign orders me to wash my hands for 60 seconds before rejoining the world of normal people. So it is a pain in the neck to go to see her.

In the second place she is vague about her history. She is not brilliant to begin with, and she has never heard of most of the diseases that the admitting form makes me ask about. Furthermore, she has picked up the idea that TB will mean extended isolation and hospitalization, so she denies all the symptoms. She calls her present illness "just a flu" but will not elaborate on how it came on. She also denies any contact with anyone who ever had TB. The intern last night discovered that her own husband was hospitalized for TB 10 years ago. When confronted with this fact, she says he never told her about it. Which may be true.

I go over the physical exam with the intern. We had a course last year on physical diagnosis, but I still do not feel capable in this field. The intern (my friend Dr. Leeds) was a student here and knows how inadequate that course was, so he takes time to go over his findings. We listen to her heart.

"She has a systolic murmur," I say. "Grade two out of six."

"Could you draw it?" he asks me.

"Yes, it would be diamond-shaped."

"Which end of the diamond is longer?" he asked me. This was a new one on me. I listened for a minute, and said, "The tail."

"I agree, but you sounded a little uncertain. You haven't heard a murmur clearly until you are ready to draw it."

He had found some slight lymph node enlargement in her neck. I had looked for it in vain.

"You can just feel it if you roll your fingers back and forth," he told me.

I rolled my fingers back and forth in the prescribed area, but came up with nothing.

"I'm sorry, I still don't feel it, and that is what I'm going to put in my write-up."

My obsessive-compulsive nature tempts me to come up with the same findings as the intern, so that there will be a correspondence between my work-up and his. In this case he will write "small cervical lymphadenopathy," and I will write "no cervical lymphadenopathy," and I feel mine has a better chance of being wrong. But I did learn one thing from my preceptor in physical diagnosis:

"Never, never say that you have seen or heard or felt something when you actually have not. If you break the rule once, slovenliness will set in and you are lost."

This is the last vestige of integrity within me, so I respect it. Besides, it's not that big a deal. If I don't feel it, I don't feel it. But I wish I did.

March 10

Lecture on EKG's. A resident in cardiology gives us a talk on a thing called "vector electrocardiography." (We are told it has been around for years, but is now becoming popular.) It seems much simpler than standard techniques: you look at 3 blimplike curves instead of 12 choppy waves. Each of the 3 curves represents the pattern of electrical forces in one dimension, so that it is very easy to spot the exact location of the myocardial infarct.* The resident puts up some simple tracings and asks us to interpret them. With a little bit of help we dope them out.

This was an exhilarating lecture because the idea is at the same time simple and fruitful. It justifies physics as a premed requirement, so that the student has at least a nodding acquaintance with vectors. A good part of medical education is background material for things that are known now and will be taught to you later; some of your education is background for things that have not yet been discovered. Vector EKG's for us are mainly a teaching device: our hospital does not routinely do them. But after fooling around with them for an hour, it is easier to understand the standard 12-lead tracings. Because vector EKG's are the Platonic forms of cardiology.

Our own resident went over a patient's standard EKG with us this afternoon. She has that mixture of good looks and gentle didacticism that I associate with my teachers in elementary school. I kidded her about this, and she told me her parents had wanted her to be a teacher, but she "foxed them." Back to EKG's.

A surgical intern who was rotating through medicine listened to the discussion with impatience. (This rotation invariably supercharges their surgical ambition.)

"There's only one thing I know about EKG's," he says.

* That is, the location of the area of injured muscle after a "heart attack."

"What's that?" I ask, playing along.
"If they're flat, that's bad."

March 11

On our ward there is a woman with leukemia. Of one kind of blood cell she has too many; of other kinds she has too few. She was treated with drugs for a year with some control, but her disease is flaring up again. We are afraid to give her more drugs for fear that we will stop all production of blood cells. She is living on transfusions of whole blood and of parts of blood.

Last night I picked up one of these transfusion units from the blood bank. It was not red but oyster white: it contained nothing but platelets, the microscopic element important in clotting. It had taken 15 units of blood to collect enough platelets for this one unit, and I estimate its price at $750. It didn't help her much.

Was it worth it?

My partner had talked to the intern and told me the party line on the subject: (1) Once you elect to treat a leukemic you have an obligation to carry him all the way. A failure of bone marrow production may be the fault of your treatment as well as the fault of the disease. (2) If this woman didn't deserve platelets, who did?

She has been in the hospital for two weeks, and we can hardly transfuse her fast enough. She is bleeding slowly and steadily into her intestinal tract. Yesterday she spiked a fever which does not respond to antibiotics, and her temperature is still rising. The fever may be due to a transfusion reaction, so we have stopped our transfusions. She continues to bleed.

On rounds we stop outside her door and her intern quietly explains the latest developments. A sickly sweet odor comes from her room and underlines his story. Also

Simon and Garfunkel's "Bridge over Troubled Waters," also sickly sweet.

One attending listens with his face set in a grimace, looking into the eyes of the other attending.

"I think we've done all we can for this poor woman."

The other attending agrees. We move on.

My new admission is not so sick. A tough, attractive young woman, with 10 days of leg pain and a week of chest pain. Her doctor put these together and suspected a pulmonary embolism: a clot from a phlebitis in the legs traveling upward and lodging in the lungs. A lung scan: a special X-ray using radioactive technique showed two areas of "decreased perfusion" on the sides of her lung fields. These were compatible with pulmonary emboli, so she was admitted.

I found her a tough customer. She could not give me a clear idea of her pains (even though she drew me a picture). And, like previous doctors, my physical exam was essentially negative. That did not rule out phlebitis and emboli, but it didn't help much.

The intern decided to take another look at her lung scan. There were two shallow indentations in the contour of her lungs: bilateral, symmetrical, only seen on the front film.

Her breasts. (She was very well endowed, and the X-ray is taken with the patient flat on her back.)

The intern checked back with the radiologist, who admitted that this was one possible interpretation.

She has very little reason to be in the hospital. We will "observe" her for a few days and then send her home. This looks like a false alarm, but it is certainly better to err on the side of safety.

March 12

The leukemic patient died this morning. We felt that she had done well for her disease, but our eventual failure must have hit her relatives hard. Loud lamentations. This was my first death this year, and I saw the contrast between the professional attitude and the real one.

The last suicide at our medical school was of a third-year student in the medical rotation some years back. The legend goes that his suicide was on the evening before Dr. Ardsley's rounds.

Today we had Dr. Ardsley's rounds.

Dr. Ardsley is the head of the Department of Medicine. His reputation for having third-year students for breakfast is exaggerated. He merely puts them in the oven.

He usually restricts himself to the big ward, and we were told to know our patients very well. I had only one patient there. She had been transferred yesterday from another part of the hospital; this was her seventh admission and her story was so complicated that her intern could barely keep it straight. My fair resident suggested that I switch patients around.

"You mean put her in a side room and put an easier patient in her place?" I asked.

"Exactly."

Sold.

I was able to talk Mrs. Portnoy into making the switch for a couple of hours. This is her fifth hospital admission, but her story is a snap in comparison. I had to move the beds myself, but 20 minutes working with my back saved me hours of mental anguish. Which is one of my aims of education.

As it turned out, Dr. Ardsley never got to that bed anyway. He started with painful slowness on the other side of the ward, where I had no patients, but I was not out of danger. He is a short, irascible man who peered at us menacingly through the upper margin of his horn-rimmed glasses. He tried to take a lot of trouble over the patient. He would have liked to catch us resting our hands on the bedrail, but we had been forewarned. He insisted on being introduced to the patient at the beginning, and then would allow the student to begin his presentation. This he never interrupted, though you could tell he was more than skeptical at certain points. When the student was finished, he would begin.

He liked to focus on the small points.

"What diet is this patient on?"

Luckily the student knew: "1200 calorie low salt."

"What does that consist of?"

"What do you mean, sir?"

Impatiently: "Describe a typical breakfast, lunch, and dinner on this regime."

The student admitted he was stumped.

"These things are important to know. How is her appetite?"

The student said he thought it was pretty good, and the patient, eager to help him, affirmed this.

"All right. What medications is this patient on?"

The student listed the medications and dosages.

"The chart records that last week the patient had a lung scan. What medication was given for this procedure?"

The student did not know. Ardsley asked the group, but we drew a blank. The resident finally answered, "Lugol's solution."

"Correct. Now would this patient's doctor tell me what is in Lugol's solution?"

Another blank.

The two hours passed very slowly and they were easily the longest in my life. He managed to make a fool out of me on the question of taking blood pressure. I said that you get a falsely low reading when you use a regular cuff on a fat person. It turns out that the reverse is true. His eyes widened when he heard my answer, so he asked me to explain the mechanism. He let me build the scaffold of pseudoscience and place the noose around my neck. When I had finished he said:

"You can't seriously believe that."

He was right. I didn't.

When it was over, we congratulated each other on our survival. It will be at least a month before we get him again, and next time we will be better prepared.

Dr. Ardsley has few fans. As a teacher he has been called the last proponent of "pedagogy through humiliation," and his coldness would keep me from recommending him as a clinician. I give him full marks, however, for trying to get across the idea that we are responsible for the sick people in our care and that we should be aware of everything we are doing to them.

Everything.

What an extraordinary idea.

March 13

We have a weekly session with a psychiatrist on the theory that there is a lot of psychiatry in internal medicine. Sensible. One of my colleagues had an old lady who had survived a heart attack a week ago and now was confined to bed rest. She didn't like bed rest, so she had to be restrained: four fabric belts kept her spread-eagled to the bed. She fought them, and in doing so probably strained her heart more than if we had let her walk about. But at least this way she would not fall and break her hip.

We tried to talk to her about the importance of bed rest after a heart attack, but we could not make contact.

"I am imprisoned. Call the police. Let me out."

She also felt that one of the attendants was trying to harm her. The psychiatrist asked her some details about

this impression, and then switched to general knowledge.
"What day is it today?"
"Monday." It was Friday.
"Who is President of the United States?"
"Kennedy."
"And who was President before Kennedy?"
"Johnson."
"And before him?"
"Truman." The woman was very sure of her answers. "You think you can trick me!"

When we were alone, the psychiatrist asked if that lady had been functioning well before her heart attack. Her student told us that she was a secretary, and had worked up to the day of her illness.

"Well now she's psychotic," the psychiatrist pointed out. "Whether this is due to her confinement we can't be sure, but this is a major diagnosis that's not on her chart."

I admitted my first acutely sick patient. Miss Evel Flanders had grown slightly jaundiced. (Her first name derived from Evelyn, but is pronounced "Evil." Her eyes were yellow, and her brown skin had an orange hue. Now there are many causes of jaundice, but hers was the most common: alcoholic cirrhosis. She had a liver that actually extended to her groin, and an abdomen that was swollen with fluid to the size of a seven-month pregnancy. She was stuporous and not yet at the stage of coma, but she would be soon.

Evel was in the intensive care unit, and we would have to work fast if we wanted her to drink again. She was dehydrated and in shock, and her potassium was dangerously low. We would have to restore her balance of fluid and electrolytes, watch out for a hypoglycemia and possible GI bleeding, and purge her gut of the normal bacterial flora whose nitrogenous wastes could push her over into coma.

I responded to this emergency by "missing" on the first IV attempt and sticking myself in the thumb on the second. The intern, Dr. Leeds, bailed me out, and put me to work doing blood tests. Up in the lab I discovered that her serum and urine unsurprisingly showed signs of jaundice, that her platelets were low and her white count was high, and that her sputum contained pneumococci. (I was surprised to find the next day that the lab technician's results agreed closely with my own.)

Dr. Leeds listened to the results with mild interest, saying, "Evel, Evel," and shaking his head. He decided that to complete the picture we needed to examine her spinal fluid and that I was to do the tap. It took me a couple of tries, but Evel was pretty out of it and I felt that any discomfort I caused her was actually therapeutic. The will to win and the intern's relaxed encouragement finally paid off: I felt the snap as the needle pierced the thick surrounding membrane and drops of clear fluid began to fall into the test tube. But it too bore the mark of Evel: it was tinged with yellow.

At midnight we felt ready to "present" to the resident. That was a first-rate experience. The resident was low-key enough to suggest it be done in the coffee shop. That was fine with us. Dr. Leeds went through the history and physical, pausing to allow the resident to copy the data in a small notebook, as he would have to present the case to *his* superior in the morning. At various points the resident would turn to me and ask a pertinent question. If I knew the answer, fine; if I didn't, he would explain it to me, and then tell the intern to continue. At the end he listened to the intern's plan of therapy, asked me some more questions about our reasons for each step, and made some suggestions of his own. There was one theoretical point we were not sure of, and he asked me to look this up.

That was a hierarchical learning experience: the intern had told me what he knew about the pathology and therapeutics of liver failure; the resident added what he had picked up in his more extensive experience, and in the morning Dr. Ardsley would teach the resident a thing or two. And after that comes God.

March 14

Evel was improved this morning. She complained about being stuck so often for blood. (Alcoholics often have very sensitive arms and legs.) I explained with just a trace of Calvinism that it was part of being in the hospital, and asked her about her drinking. She explained she was just a social drinker. On her last admission she had set her consumption at a pint to a quart daily for several days a week for 20 years. Usually port, but whiskey when she could get it. Her favorite: J & B.

Apart from drawing blood, my only other responsibility to patients is planting tuberculin tests, or PPD's.* This is conventionally done on the forearm, and it should be injected not under the skin but superficially, to form a blister. A reaction around the site indicates that the patient has been exposed to tuberculosis; it does not always signify active or latent disease. But if it is positive, the diagnosis of TB should be considered a little more seriously, and TB is so protean that it should be included in the differential diagnosis of nearly every case on this ward (except perhaps the heart attacks). There is a hospital rule that is rarely obeyed that PPD's should be done on every patient. The medical service is fairly compulsive about it, because if we miss the diagnosis we really feel stupid. Antibiotics have made TB much less common now, and that is why it is criminal to miss it.

There are three concentrations of PPD—listed as first, intermediate, and second strength. Most patients get the intermediate. If you suspect the patient has active TB, start out slow with the first strength; if he does not react,

* PPD = purified protein derivative (tuberculin).

you move up to the intermediate, and finally to the second strength.

Before administering the test I check through the charts. On one admission I noted that the patient had tested positive six years ago. That meant I should start out slow. I looked around for some first strength but couldn't find any. I could have searched the whole hospital, but I had a hundred other things to do, so I gave her the standard intermediate strength.

As soon as I had injected it I had pangs of conscience, because I knew that it is possible for a patient to overreact, with actual sloughing of the skin. I talked to Dr. Leeds about it.

"Have you ever injected intradermal cortisone?" he asked me.

"No."

"Well, you may have to do it." He smiled.

I watched the site of injection anxiously. God was good, and at the end of two days there was only a minimal reaction: a small area of swelling, measuring 9 mm.

Dr. Leeds told me that 8 mm or above meant a positive reaction. I recorded it as such in the chart.

The next day the resident told me that the reaction had to be 10 mm to be positive, and that I should move up to second strength.

I did what I was told to.

And the day after, the nurse told me that patient was complaining about her arm.

The new site had swelled to the size of half a lemon. And there were little red tracks going up her arm.

I called in the intern. We are both mad at the resident for ordering the second strength; I am mad at myself for not questioning it. And we are both scared.

March 15

The reaction seems to have been contained by cold soaks and topical cream. We were lucky, but I never want to have to be lucky again. Not over a PPD.

March 16

Evel is still complaining about blood tests and wants to know when she can go home. Not for a while, dear. (At least not while your eyes are still yellow.)

I was down in the intensive care unit writing my notes on Evel. All the patients down there seem pretty sick, but I noticed one woman was sitting upright in her bed and breathing fast. I went over and asked her how she was doing.

"So, so."

There were plenty of nurses around and none of them seemed concerned, so I decided that this was about par for the ICU and returned to my write-up.

I worked for five minutes and then was startled to see the "crash cart" being rushed to her bed.

It was a cardiac arrest.

Within 60 seconds the whole arrest team was there, including the cardiologist (who has to carry a portable EKG machine wherever he goes), the anesthesiologist, the medical interns, and some nurses who actually knew where to find things. The syringes had been previously drawn up and labeled, and everything was where it should be. The doctors wanted her chest X-ray, so I went down to radiology to retrieve it. When I returned with it four minutes later, her heart was beating and her EKG looked normal to me.

I still felt stupid for not using my stethoscope ten minutes earlier.

She was felt to be stable, and the team dispersed. One intern was monitoring her. An hour later, she arrested again.

Dr. Leeds was on duty from our ward. "It must be one of those nights," he shouted as he ran to the bed and started pumping her chest.

She was responding to the second round of emergency procedures. The loudspeaker that had summoned everyone to the arrest now announced, "An urgent page for Dr. Leeds, an urgent page for Dr. Leeds."

Dr. Leeds looked up. "I told you it was going to be one of those nights." Another intern took over his job of pumping her chest, and Leeds was like a vision of his culture hero Groucho as he tore down the hall, his body low, his long legs telescoping, with two medical students/clowns close on his heels. (He already has the requisite glasses and moustache.) The family of the patient who arrested were amazed to think that there was another emergency in the hospital so acute that doctors had to leave their relative's bedside to attend to it. Dr. Leeds flew up the stairs to his ward, ready for anything.

The nurse told him that his new admission had vomited.

She couldn't understand why we thought it was so funny. I decided that since I was not on duty I would do best to leave.

March 17

As in pediatrics, we have preceptor sessions in the medical rotation, and this is where the real teaching goes on. We meet three afternoons a week—five students and one preceptor, and the size of the group makes it difficult to conceal one's ignorance. In each session we go through one of about twenty major afflictions that come under the province of internal medicine, and we are expected to know the pathology, symptoms, diagnosis, treatment, and latest esoterica. This information can be found in a textbook of medicine and a recent comprehensive article in a medical journal. Our preceptor is a hard-minded "doc" who divides his time between cancer research and a medical clinic. He has a way of twitching his nose and sniffing when he detects bullshit or uncertainty. He feels that medicine is straightforward enough that there is no excuse for not getting it right the first time. We found medicine a little more complicated than that, but it was within the bounds of learnability.

Our preceptor also goes over our write-ups of each admission. Compulsive is hardly the word for these. Exhaustive might be better, because of its effect on both parties. After the chief complaint, you have to record the family medical history (complete with a family tree), a personal history (down to the average number of cups of coffee), and a social history (noting what floor the apartment is on and whether there is an elevator). Then comes the previous health and illnesses, and the litany of "Did you ever have . . ." You ask them fast and hope they answer "no" to each of these questions, because a "yes" compels you to "describe in detail": what were the symptoms, when they first appeared, how they were evaluated and treated, and when was the last recurrence. Old people tended to answer in the affirmative.

With this background, you can now approach the "present illness." This is the hardest part, because there is no check list, and you are on your own. Listing "the symptoms in order of appearance" can be difficult: at what point do complaints become "symptoms"? Did the "flu" 3 weeks ago have anything to do with this illness? And which appeared first, the night sweats or the flank pain? One refinement I admire is that you are supposed to guess the probable disease and to list the symptoms that the patient did *not* have. (That is really ingenious.)

Next, the physical. Also exhaustive. Then the summary of positive findings. And finally the provisional diagnosis (or diagnoses, since the average patient had at least three diseases) with a list of other possibilities to be "ruled out." Your signature and the date, which should be within 24 hours of the patient's admission. It was usually later.

I feel that my whole third year prepared me to do this write-up, and I think that I do it well. Whatever my preceptor says. He returns each work-up with corrections which at first seem petty but later can be viewed as small-minded. I get annoyed: too many corrections and I have to recopy the whole thing in a final compulsive gesture. But I will admit that this is the last time that anyone will take the trouble to read my work-ups with care and to force me to be careful. My write-ups averaged five pages; the interns' were two or three. They turned them out faster, but mine were more complete. And mine can only get more like theirs as time goes on. If you are going downhill, start high.

March 18

The cardiac monitor unit reminds me of the command room of a guided missile destroyer I once visited. A continuous EKG machine spits forth a seamless web of ten-track tracings, clattering like a frenetic longhand teletype. Ten orange-faced oscilloscopes allow the nurses to see instantaneously what each patient's ticker is up to; and should there be any questions, a bank of ten Sony TV's record the grosser movements in each room. Daytime TV, real-life hospital drama: ten silent patients zonked out, aged and mostly overweight, looking like flipped sea turtles. Occasionally a nurse appears on screen, but there is no audio unless she presses the intercom.

"SQUAWK. We're taking Mr. Jones off the pacer for a second, so don't worry. END SQUAWK."

Mr. Jones's oscilloscope begins to show lightning patterns. A soft buzzer bleeps, and a red light on it flashes. But nobody pays it no mind, and soon the normal monotony returns.

A patient who had "arrested" in another part of the hospital was transferred to this unit. I was on duty, so I "picked her up." I never really got to know her, because she was on a respirator from the start and never said a word. She never even looked at me.

"This lady did one important thing tonight," the intern told me.

"What's that?"

"She received the Last Sacrament."

We knew we were in for a nightful of work, and we had few illusions about the outcome.

My job was to draw the blood and do the initial hematology tests. My roommate was working in the lab tonight, so I got him to do the tests. This left me free to draw blood. Since she was on a respirator, we had to follow her arterial blood gases closely. All my previous blood-taking had been from veins, and arteries are much harder to hit as they are smaller, deeper, and tougher. I had tried once or twice on Evel, but her crying would unsettle me and the intern would have to finish the job. Tonight the intern was too busy and this patient was guaranteed not to cry.

I was told it was OK to go for the femorals. The usual location for getting arterial blood is the arm or the wrist. The femorals are a second choice because (a) if you miss you might hurt the femoral nerve, and (b) some patients do not like a needle anywhere near their groin. Again, the lady was too far gone for either contraindication.

You find the pulse, place two fingers on it, and roll them back and forth until you are sure that they straddle the line of maximum impulse, then you go in. You can tell if you are getting arterial blood by its bright red color, in contrast to the venous crimson. It always looks beautiful, because it spells success. You place the syringe in ice and press a gauze pad to the artery for five minutes, to make sure that the bleeding has stopped. Then you rush the sample to the lab, where a simplified Japanese machine takes about 40 seconds to tell you the pH and the concentrations of O_2 and CO_2. Some other values are calculated by inference from these three figures, and in a total of 10 minutes, start to finish, you have your results.

I had to do this four times, so I became pretty good at drawing arterial blood gases, at least on this woman. At 7 AM the intern tried and missed, and I bailed him out.

"MacNab, you learned something tonight."

I told him I owed this woman a month's tuition, and he laughed.

I was able to connect on Evel's wrist for her morning blood gases, so I really do feel I have learned something. Again, stemming from previous success, the Will to Win.

One of the interns referred today to our hospital as "Big Sky General." That struck me as a good name for this place. I thought he was alluding to its tall buildings and ivory tower aspects. I learned that he had something else in mind.

"When I was in medical school," he explained, "I did my fourth-year medicine in a suburban hospital. On Sundays the attending used to come to rounds in Bermuda shorts and golf shoes. He would practice his putting stance while we were presenting. One time we had finished our reports on each of the patients in a small ward. As we turned to go, the attending pointed to an empty bed and asked about the patient who had been there yesterday. The resident hesitated and, realizing that the other patients were listening, replied that he had been transferred.

"The euphemism went right by the attending. 'Transferred? That guy looked critically ill.'

" 'Yes, sir,' said the resident. 'Transferred to Big Sky General.' "

So there is in this nickname a whiff of a Singapore death house and a tad of a germ-free heaven which, when combined with the tall buildings and the ivory tower, make it a very good nickname indeed.

March 19

The walls of the patients' rooms in the cardiac monitor unit are decorated with travel posters. Color pictures of California, New York, Mexico, and Bermuda—perhaps to give these people a reason for reviving, or maybe to add some glamour to death. They do make these rooms a lot more cheerful.

It was decided today to catheterize this woman's heart to see what the pressure was in the region of her lungs. This is important to know in determining how much IV fluid you should give: if the pressure is high you will give less, and low more.

The procedure was carried out in a room that was more like a lab than an operating theater. Gowns, masks, and sterile technique were employed, but the electronic equipment set the dominant tone. All we wanted was a few numbers.

The catheter was guided in and out of the heart by means of fluoroscopy: a TV screen showed the cinematic X-ray of the pumping heart and the long snaking wire that we were trying to tease through. It was like watching a broadcast from the moon: the transmission was poor, but the subject was pretty fantastic.

I had a talk with Evel's cousin, who attributed that woman's alcoholism to "bad company" and promised to keep her from drinking in the future. This cousin is a good woman, and I will care more about Evel because she cares about her. Internal medicine is mainly caring for people who eat too much, drink too much, smoke too much, and exercise too little, and it is very easy to get the idea that illness is deserved. There are two other big groups—heart conditions and cancer beyond surgery—and with these people you tend to reflect that a fairly full life has been lived. It looks as if this field has fewer satisfactions than most others.

March 20

I got up at 3 AM to prepare a presentation on Evel for attending rounds this morning. I do not plan to make a habit of such early risings, but a lot had happened. I had been up for two days and I had to have some sleep. This way I could work when the hospital was quiet, and I would have time only to memorize the important things.

I divided my time between her chart and the textbook. At 7 AM I went to draw the required blood samples for tests on my patients. I discovered there were no bloods to draw on my lady in the monitor unit, as she had "checked out" overnight. Technically the first patient I have lost, but I didn't care, as it was a foregone conclusion. I was glad to have some extra time for my presentation.

Today's attending was the opposite of Dr. Ardsley: he likes students and he likes to teach in a slow-talking, relaxed but expert fashion. He concentrates on differential diagnosis. He let the first student give his presentation sentence by sentence: as each symptom appeared he would ask, "What diseases does this suggest?" and he would go around the room and get an answer from each of us. The student who was presenting was not on the spot: the audience was. The one presentation lasted two hours, so I was off the hook (although I had learned something in the preparation). At the end, he went around the room again, and asked each of us to name the one thing he had learned in this session, by way of reinforcement. A modest goal and a successful one. His main point is that you should think of as many diseases as possible in your differential, and that way you are less likely to miss the unusual ones.

Since I have been on medicine I have avoided going anywhere for dinner, but we are close to spring vacation and I felt I could relax this rule. I was in a mood for celebrating, because I am nearly one-quarter through this rotation and I feel I have already come up against the worst. I went to dinner at the home of my great-uncle, a partner in a law firm, where I was pleased to find some Campari. He told me amusing stories about the defense of the cigarette companies in suits involving lung cancer. (These suits are usually brought by the widows of smokers who had died from that ailment. The plaintiff is usually poor and black. If you can prove that her husband had been previously married and never divorced, you thus deprive her of a basis for a lawsuit.) I once again congratulate myself on escaping the clutches of the law.

He is a very bright man and could have done anything. He asked me to describe a typical day, and I complied, but I couldn't begin to communicate the frustration or the excitement. He listened with interest, and I got the feeling that he felt he could have risen to a senior partnership in this field if he had gone into it. I'm sure he could have. The professions are all interchangeable in that "talent" plays a minor role: the basic requirements are a marginal amount of brains and some training—the experience comes free.

"What field are you going into?"

I told him I still wasn't sure.

"I hope it's general practice, and I hope that you come to Kent [his country place] to work. We are so short of doctors that for years nobody has been born in our county

—all the babies are delivered in the city, forty miles away. I'll even guarantee your practice."

I told him I would think about it. My range of choice is big, and I don't want to pin myself down. But it's nice to have an offer.

March 23

Most admissions demand a lot of work with very little teaching in return. After an evening of drawing blood samples, running them over to the lab, doing some tests yourself, taking an EKG and cutting and taping the strips in the chart, and tracking down the chest X-ray, all in addition to the scut work for the rest of the ward, you are tempted to ask why you are paying tuition.

Tonight I got some teaching. We admitted a patient suffering from a prolonged asthmatic attack. The initial work-up was complete, and the intern suggested I write some orders, just for practice.

"And don't peek at my order sheet."

I looked up "asthma" in a textbook of medicine and studied the section on treatment. A few specific drugs and dosages, which I copied onto my sheet. The intern saw that I was not getting very far.

"It's possible to begin every set of orders the same way. First write down 'Admit to Ward ___,' and then remember 'Don't Call Alvin Dad Violet.'"

This turns out to be a mnemonic:

Don't = Diagnosis (even a tentative one)
Call = Condition (either "satisfactory" or "poor"; "good" is like asking for trouble)
Alvin = Activity ("bed rest," "bed rest with bathroom privileges," etc.)
Dad = Diet (the varieties are endless, the results the same)

Violet = Vital signs (temperature, pulse, blood pressure, and weight, and how often each of these should be checked)

"Now for medications. I find it useful to write orders for the little things first, like aspirin, milk of magnesia (MOM), mineral oil, and a light sedative. This way I won't get awakened because Mr. Jones feels constipated or has a pain in his left big toe or is afraid he can't get to sleep. [The mnemonic here is "Bed, Board, Bowels, and Bufferin."]
"Now for treating the asthma, always remember:
>   Hydrate
>   Aerate
>   Sedate

"In practice I never sedate, but it's a good thing to keep at the back of your mind. Now, what are you going to hydrate her with?"

I found that once he gave me the key, the book and I could come up with satisfactory answers. In this way we covered all the medications, respirators, IV solutions, and further lab tests.

For the first time I understood exactly what was being done for a patient and why. As with directions, you have to drive there or you don't really know the way.

March 24

Our psychiatry preceptor asked us to recommend patients for an interview. I suggested Mrs. Portnoy. ("Doctor, I'm asking you, what's wrong with me? I'm falling apart!") Unfortunately she was out, being treated to yet another diagnostic procedure.

One student told about a patient of his who had leukemia but had not been told so in that many words. Last night she had seen on TV a hospital drama about a girl with the same symptoms as she who turned out to have leukemia. She was still upset. We decided she would not be a good patient to interview.

We settled on a woman with nephritis—a straight "medical" disease, with no psychiatric overtones. She had a private room. Her radio was playing when we came in, and nobody asked her to turn it off. The whole interview took place to appropriate music. It was much more natural that way, like listening to someone in a bar. She was a little reluctant to talk about her unhappiness, but our preceptor wanted to make the point that it had something to do with her disease, and gently questioned her. It turned out that her father had died two months before, and that she had been clinically depressed since then, without giving free range to her grief. The psychiatrist said that there just might be a connection between the two, and that often it was better to let your feelings out. The radio echoed this advice with:

> *Let it be, let it be*
> *Let it be, let it be.*
> *Whisper words of wisdom*
> *Let it be, let it be.*

The point was made.

Afterward, the psychiatrist warned us about the danger of "grooving on" * a patient's story. I realized I had been doing just this during the preceding hour. It was Friday afternoon, and I was tired, and this is the next best thing to going to sleep. But under any circumstances I find it very easy to slip into this form of listening, and I resolved to cut it out. At least on the job.

Before leaving for a brief vacation, I tried to check a chest X-ray on a patient as a favor to the intern. I looked all around the radiology files for the plate and checked the records for the past two days. Nothing. I returned to

---

* "Grooving on": enjoying an experience in a dissociated way. Unprofessional in the extreme.

the ward and asked the nurses what time this patient had gone for the procedure. It turned out she had never been sent, and this oversight would be remedied as soon as possible. Final prevacation frustration—and there will be more waiting for me when I return to finish up this rotation (which also finishes up the year).

I had a chance to cheat the commuter railroad on the way to my family's home, but I didn't. We live on one of the farthest stops on our line. My brother had told me that if you buy a ticket to the first station you can ride the rest of the way free. I was eager to try this, partly out of curiosity and because I didn't think I would have enough money to get home. I have never felt that morally I owed this railroad anything for my use of it: by rights I would be entitled to a payment for its abuse of me. But I was restrained by the thought that I am practically a doctor, and it would not look very good if I were caught.

Such is my confirmation into the bourgeoisie.

One of the important questions about the third year is why have I put up with it. The easiest answer is that it gets me into fourth year. Except for a month of psychiatry and a month of vacation, the entire fourth year is elective. An advisor dissuades you from spending the entire time on the beach by reminding you that your internship comes at the end. (That could be the best reason for spending it on the beach.)

The schedule that I am asking for:

JUNE Pediatrics, subinternship

JULY
AUGUST Medicine in the tropics (hopefully
SEPTEMBER Thailand)

OCTOBER Work in a research lab

NOVEMBER Psychiatry

DECEMBER	Medicine subinternship (in a hospital
JANUARY	without interns to follow around)
FEBRUARY	Radiology
MARCH	Surgery
APRIL	Ophthalmology
MAY	Obstetrics/Gynecology

It all looks great on paper. It might even turn out that way. The best thing about it is that I have chosen it myself. Nobody else my age or any age has that range of freedom in deciding how he is to spend the next 12 months. I am required to stick to the medicine business more or less, but I have the choice of any hospital in this city, any city in this country, and almost any country in the world (except Red China). I will stay in this city for the most part, except for my trip to Thailand. And to get there and back, I will have to go around the world. This will be very expensive (costing around $2000, which I do not have) but I figure that you are a fourth-year student only once. And then the system has a way of closing in.

Off-Service Note

Another thing that has a way of closing in is this journal. I am finding it harder and harder to maintain this double role of skeptical observer and credulous participant, and I find that as the year has progressed the material seems to come less from my life and training and more from the patient's misfortune. The story about the girl with leukemia and the TV program has left me with increasing misgivings, and I hope none of my patients confront themselves here.

I have not been the perfect third-year student; such students have no time for journals. I kept a journal—I thought this would be a pivotal year in my development toward a reasonable facsimile of a doctor (or that it would document my change of heart in case I couldn't carry through). It was originally intended for my friends and grandchildren, but as I began to appreciate the ignorance about what goes on in medical school, I began to think more about letting others read it as well. I had strong reservations about publication, particularly considering betrayal of confidence.

I have compromised by changing most of the proper nouns, including my own name. I concede that this is a cop-out of the first order. Here are some excuses:

(1) I want to protect the hospital, which I still revere. I send my family there to get fixed up, and if I ever get sick, that is where I will head. I may have written about its failures, but what I saw was mainly success.

(2) I want to protect my medical school, which accepted me on a bet and has worked hard to teach me something. I am grateful.

(3) I want to protect myself; I do not want to tie up the rest of my life in litigation.

But most of all, I want to be a doctor.